Conan Doyle

£ 2·70

CONAN DOYLE

❖

MICHAEL COREN

BLOOMSBURY

First published in Great Britain 1995

This paperback edition 1996

Bloomsbury Publishing Plc, 38 Soho Square, London W1V 5DF

Copyright © 1995 by Michael Coren

The moral right of the author has been asserted

PICTURE SOURCES

All pictures are supplied courtesy of Richard Lancelyn Green

A CIP catalogue record for this book is
available from the British Library

ISBN 0 7475 2668 0

10 9 8 7 6 5 4 3 2 1

Typeset by Hewer Text Composition Services, Edinburgh
Printed in Great Britain by Cox & Wyman Ltd, Reading

Contents

To Helen and Stephen

Acknowledgements

With a book of this nature there are numerous people to thank and I ask for their forgiveness if any of those who helped me with this one do not find their names here. My gratitude to the following: David Frum, Dean Godson, Paul Goodman, David Reynolds, Bruce Westwood, Lucinda Vardey; and to Carolyn Brunton, the late Julian Symons, John Murray, Aidan Mackey, the Earl of Longford, Francis Wheen, John Hayes, Dorothy and the late David Regan, Greg Gatenby, Richard Lancelyn Green, Kate Filion, Daniel Richler, the British Library of Political and Economic Science, the London School of Economics and Political Science, the Library of St Michael's College, University of Toronto, the G.K. Chesterton papers, formerly at Top Meadow, now in the British Library in London, the Harry Ransom Humanities Center at the University of Texas at Austin, the library of Edinburgh University and the public library system of the city of Edinburgh, Iain Benson, the National Sound Archive, Professor Norman Sherry, Penny Phillips, Richard Dawes, the Hilaire Belloc collection at Boston College, Massachusetts, the staff at the library at the University of Nottingham, the Scottish Catholic History Society, the Spiritualist Society of Great Britain. And, of course, my wife Bernadette. As always.

Introduction

We who are interested in the life of Arthur Conan Doyle are very fortunate people. By contrast with so many intriguing and beguiling figures from the past, even the recent past, there is film footage of Conan Doyle – speaking, laughing, gesticulating, just moving. How a person holds limbs and head, how a body moves and how a face gestures, are aspects of a life that no amount of research among papers and letters can genuinely illuminate. Because of this, and for many other reasons as well, we are indeed very fortunate people.

The best, longest footage of Conan Doyle was filmed by Fox-Case Movietone in 1929; it was produced and directed by Jack Connolly, photographed by Ben Miggins and sound was by Harry Squires, D.F. Whiting and Harry Kaw. It is eleven and a half minutes long and includes only two figures: Arthur Conan Doyle and his dog. The former steals the show.

The piece begins with a statement from the makers. 'William Fox has the honour to present the world-famous author and scientist Sir Arthur Conan Doyle.' Rather grandiloquent music follows, and then: 'Sir Arthur Conan Doyle is famous the world over for his Sherlock Holmes stories. He has devoted the past forty years to spiritualistic study and is one of the leading advocates of the existence of spirit life and communication with the beyond.' As soon as Conan Doyle comes into shot, walking down a set of grassy steps, he begins his flirtation with the camera. He removes his hat, puts a book on a small table and explains that he has been asked to say a few words so as to test the recording equipment. Considering the novelty of film at that time and the inexperience of Conan Doyle before the camera, he is a consummate performer. He appears to be ironic, tongue-in-cheek, always one step ahead of the audience. He is almost playing with us, this sprightly and youthful seventy-year-old. He walks to the front of a gnarled old tree and sits down. There is a monocle hanging from the top button of his tightly wrapped double-breasted jacket. We see a tiredness about his eyes, signs of age, and he coughs occasionally. His accent is still melodious, softly Scottish, careful, deliberate. The film fades in and out with the sunlight, giving a strange, otherworldly feel and ambience.

Conan Doyle might as well be establishing the outline of his life's work when he says in the preamble to his talk: 'there are two things that people always ask me; one is how I came to write the Sherlock Holmes stories, the other is about how I came to have psychic experiences and to take so much interest in that question.' He explains that as a young doctor he had time on his hands and read detective stories but was invariably annoyed and frustrated by the denouements of the books. Either the crimes were solved by flukes or the solutions were left unexplained, and 'that didn't seem to me quite playing the game'. Conan Doyle explains that because of this, and because of his medical training, he decided to adapt scientific methods to deduction. He describes his old teacher in Edinburgh, Dr Bell, who possessed extraordinary powers of observation and who could ascertain any number of things about patients simply by looking at them. 'I thought of a hundred little dodges as you may say,' he explains of his inchoate detective creation, 'a hundred little touches by which he could build up his conclusions'.

He concludes his discussion of Sherlock Holmes by saying that initially people took little interest in the stories but soon changed their mind and that was all to the good for them as well as for him. He also says that he has written more than he wanted to about Holmes and Watson but that 'my hand has been forced' and this 'monstrous growth has come out of what was really a comparatively small seed'. He emphasizes that Holmes is not a real person and smiles as he mentions those correspondents who write to Holmes, care of the author. How he wishes that they would leave him alone.

But then he moves on to what for him is clearly a more interesting and important subject, spiritualism, and he almost dismisses Holmes as a distraction. He looks directly into the camera as he recalls his first spiritualist wanderings in 1886 and 1887 – at the same time, in fact, as the early development of Sherlock Holmes. He states that he will not write any more Holmes stories but that his psychic interest grows ever stronger; he wishes to be a missionary, to spread the good news to other people 'less fortunate' than himself who have not yet heard the good news, to use his position as a public figure to be 'a gramophone on the subject', meeting people and trying to make them understand. Spiritualism is, says this charming, avuncular man, 'the basis for all religious improvement in the human race'. But then he changes character, becomes more forthright and even a little aggressive. He has sat with an enormous number and variety of mediums all over the world, he says, and does not like people contradicting him when they know nothing of the subject. 'When I talk on this subject I'm not talking about what I believe, I'm not talking about what I think, I'm talking about what I know.'

The speech ends on a moving note. Conan Doyle explains that he has never allowed fraud or hallucination to blur his experiences and has always had witnesses and proof when he has been with mediums. 'It was only in the time of the war when all these splendid young fellows were disappearing from our view,' he says, that he became completely convinced that spiritualism was all-important. He adds that he has received so many letters from people who have been consoled by spiritualism that he could fill a room in his house with them.

Then he pauses, stands up, picks up his trilby-type hat and a book, says a simple 'Goodbye' and 'Come along' to his dog and retreats up the stone stairs. He would be dead within a year. Or, in his terms, would simply have disappeared from view.

This is a biographical study of Conan Doyle rather than an orthodox literary biography. The latter has already been tackled, in some form or other and with varying degrees of success, and the groundwork of research and work has already been done, principally by such scholars as Owen Dudley Edwards. There is a fundamental problem facing anyone writing of the life of Arthur Conan Doyle: that of the collection of the man's papers housed in Switzerland that are not currently open for analysis to any researcher or biographer. This collection could, of course, contain nothing of particular importance, yet it might well be of profound significance. Either way, it must not, cannot, stop us from bringing new perspectives to bear on so fascinating a character.

In his autobiography, *Memories and Adventures*, published in 1924, Conan Doyle wrote a brief but telling preface. It is a useful conspectus of his life and shows the order of importance in which he himself listed his achievements and accomplishments. Those Sherlockian monomaniacs who remain convinced, or pretend to be convinced, that Sherlock Holmes was a real figure and that Conan Doyle's life was important only so far as it touched on Holmes, would do well to read the introduction before bed, every night. Conan Doyle's reputation would benefit and so would they.

INTRODUCTION

'I have had a life which, for variety and romance, could, I think, hardly be exceeded. I have known what it was to be a poor man and I have known what it was to be fairly affluent. I have sampled every kind of human experience. I have known many of the most remarkable men of my time. I have had a long literary career after a medical training which gave me the M.D. of Edinburgh. I have tried my hand at very many sports, including boxing, cricket, billiards, motoring, football, aeronautics and ski-ing, having been the first to introduce the latter for long journeys into Switzerland. I have travelled as Doctor to a whaler for seven months in the Arctic and afterwards in the West Coast of Africa. I have seen something of three wars, the Soudanese, the South African and the German. My life has been dotted with adventures of all kinds. Finally I have been constrained to devote my latter years to telling the world the final result of thirty-six years' study of the occult, and in endeavouring to make it realize the overwhelming importance of the question. In this mission I have already travelled more than 50,000 miles and addressed 300,000 people, besides writing seven books upon the subject.'

No mention of the bulk of his writing and no mention at all of Sherlock Holmes or Dr Watson. Here is Conan Doyle the doctor, Conan Doyle the adventurer, Conan Doyle the journalist and, above all, Conan Doyle the spiritualist. The intention of the present book is to describe Conan Doyle the man, the composite of all of these aspects and of many more. As one of his creations once said, 'It is quite a three-pipe problem . . .'

1

A Scottish Childhood

Arthur Ignatius Conan Doyle was born in a flat in Picardy Place, Edinburgh, on 22 May 1859. A short way to the east of Conan Doyle's first home is Carlton Hill; just a little further to the west is the city's famous Princes Street. All around the wide, short road, then and now, are monuments and streets named after historical figures, literary and military heroes. The street of his birth was given its name by Huguenots who had settled there and Conan Doyle was interested in and sympathetic towards these French Protestants all his life, later using them as protagonists in a novel.

Indeed history, the events and people that shaped the world, permeated Conan Doyle's life from an early age. He always felt himself to be close to those who had lived before him, and had a strong historical consciousness. Part of this was due to his growing up in Edinburgh, a city soaked in history, but also to the influence of his mother, Mary Doyle. 'Her father was a young doctor of Trinity College, William Foley, who died young and left his family in comparative poverty,' Conan Doyle wrote in his autobiography. 'He had married one Katherine Pack, whose death-bed – or rather the white waxen thing which lay upon that bed – is the very earliest recollection of my life. Her near relative – uncle, I think – was Sir Denis Pack, who led the Scottish brigade at Waterloo.' The family traced its Irish line from an officer in Oliver Cromwell's settling army, and one of the seventeenth-century Packs, the Reverend Richard, head of Kilkenny College, married Mary Percy and thus formed a link with the royal Plantagene family. It was certainly a tenuous relationship but, typical of Conan Doyle's mother and to a large extent of Conan Doyle himself, one that was spoken about in personal, almost intimate terms. Grandeur without substance. Mary Foley was a snob, compensating for her lack of position in her own time with references to familial glories from long ago. Harmless, understandable but still most annoying to her friends and neighbours.

This strong-willed, intelligent and charismatic woman was the youngest daughter of the Katherine Pack whom Conan Doyle had remembered in her death, an Irish Roman Catholic who had come to Edinburgh when her husband had died. She left her homeland for economic reasons, fearing that in Ireland she could not keep her family together. In Edinburgh she became a landlady, letting out a room in her flat. From rent, part-time work and a small inheritance she managed to send the twelve-year-old Mary, the centre of her life, away to a school in France, where she hoped that the girl would receive not only a good education but a solid grounding in Catholicism. She was given both.

Charles Doyle was also a Catholic, also intelligent and also, thanks to being a paying tenant, resident in Katherine Pack's home in the early 1850s. He fell for Katherine's daughter, the 'bright-eyed, very intelligent' Mary, from the very beginning of his stay even though the girl was only a teenager.[1] Katherine Pack was never completely happy with this, not only because of her daughter's age but because she didn't quite approve of her young tenant. Katherine had invested love and, particularly, money into the girl and although she didn't know who exactly she wanted to be her son-in-law she was sure Charles Doyle was not him. And it was in his character that Charles would not mind this a bit.

Charles Altamont Doyle's family were of Anglo-Norman origin and Charles's father, John, had come to London from Dublin in 1815. For more than a quarter of a century, up until the 1850s, John Doyle made his name, and a famous name, as the caricaturist 'H.B.'. His success lay in a departure from the glorious grotesques of the eighteenth century, of Gillray and Rowlandson, and the invention of a cleaner, more courteous and accurate portrait of politicians, authors, soldiers and the like. Soldiers he particularly enjoyed drawing and it was said at the time that this was because he bore such a striking resemblance to the Duke of Wellington and was even saluted in parks and streets as he strolled along. He did nothing to discourage these tributes. When he died in 1868, John Doyle was mourned by far more than his immediate family. By any standard Conan Doyle's paternal grandfather's life was a great triumph.

John Doyle had married Marianna Conan, the sister of another artist, Michael Conan, and between them they had seven children, two girls and five boys. Richard was the most successful, becoming the main cartoonist for *Punch* and designing a cover for the magazine that remained in use until the 1940s. James became an author and wrote, among others, *A Chronicle of England and the Official Baronage of England*. Francis died in his teens. Henry painted professionally and also worked as an art critic, becoming director of the National Gallery of Ireland in 1869. His purchases for the gallery, and his administration of it, were enlightened, original and intensely successful. He is fondly remembered to this day.

So both father and brothers had given Charles Doyle a challenge, one that was difficult to emulate. For him things had started well, however. The reason he was in Scotland was that a position had been found for him by his father as a clerk and architect in the Office of Works in Edinburgh. The job was that of a civil servant and bureaucrat, profoundly different from those of most of his brothers. He was paid £240 a year for this dreary and unfulfilling work and managed to supplement his income by around £60 a year by selling the pictures he painted in his free time. This was frustrated talent and frustrated ambition. The situation was not helped by the letters Charles received from his brothers telling him of their dinners with famous London characters, of the vibrant social scene and of the sheer enjoyment they were experiencing. They were creative people doing creative things. His sense of isolation increased with every letter and he longed to return home. His son Arthur remembered the letters he wrote, referring to Scottish society as being 'rough' and 'hard-drinking', and 'into which he had been precipitated at a dangerously early age, especially for one with his artistic temperament. He had some fine religious instincts, but his environment was a difficult one.'[2] This is an example of kindness and of filial loyalty.

Times were extremely difficult for Charles Doyle, who was often very unhappy and turned increasingly to alcohol to ease and shorten those long hours and days of loneliness and bitterness. 'He was quite unambitious and no great promotion ever came his way,' wrote Conan Doyle of his father. 'His painting was done spasmodically and the family did not always reap the benefit, for Edinburgh is full of water-colours which he had given away.' Again, unfulfilled and unhappy.

Mary changed a great deal of that. She was pretty, with grey eyes and fair hair, and could, when she wanted, be exceedingly charming. It was a marriage, however, made less in heaven than one provoked by the desperation of a very sad man and the naive excitement of an impressionable and romantic young woman. Charles and Mary married in 1855, when Mary was just seventeen. The young woman's hobby was, of all things, heraldry: 'The Doyles, I grant you, are gentlefolk of ancient lineage,' she would protest. 'But we, on the other hand, are descended from the house of Plantagenet.' There would be trouble ahead.

The first of the couple's children was Annette, a neglected

girl who died when she was a young woman. She had been sent off as a governess to Portugal as soon as was possible and was obliged to send almost all her income back to Scotland to help her parents and siblings. Catherine came next, in 1858, but she died in infancy. Arthur was the third child, and the name Conan was inserted at the behest of Charles Doyle's uncle and Arthur's godfather, Michael Conan, who insisted that he be commemorated at the boy's christening. Mary was born in 1861 but also died in childhood, as did another girl, Caroline, born in 1866. Constance was born the following year; Lottie, known as Caroline, in 1869 and Innes, the only other boy in the family, in 1873. The last two children were Ida, born in 1875, and Bryan Mary, born in 1877.

With Arthur, their first son, both parents were delighted. He was a happy baby who laughed a lot and cried little. He walked early and could speak in short sentences by the time he was two and a half. He was always very attached to his mother, calling for her when he was hurt and falling asleep in her lap until he was five or six. An inventive little boy, he would transform his games of hide-and-seek into historical adventures and ancient battles. And he would ask his parents questions for hours on end – at least it seemed that long to them. How many people live in that country? Where is that place? Who made this? Why was that done? His infant years were a time of happiness despite his parents' lack of money. Young Arthur was an attractive, pleasing boy and his mother, and to a certain extent his father, spent as much time with him as they could. He was a favourite.

'Of my boyhood I need say little, save that it was Spartan at home and more Spartan at the Edinburgh school where a tawse-brandishing schoolmaster of the old type made our young lives miserable,' wrote Conan Doyle.[3] 'From the age of seven to nine I suffered under this pock-marked, one-eyed rascal who might have stepped from the pages of Dickens. In the evenings, home and books were my sole consolation, save for week-end holidays. My comrades were rough boys and I became a rough boy, too. If there is any truth in the idea of reincarnation – a point on which my mind is still open – I think some earlier experience of mine must have been as a stark fighter, for it came out strongly in youth, when I rejoiced in battle. We lived for some time in a cul de sac street with a very vivid life of its own and a fierce feud between the small boys who dwelt on either side of it. Finally it was fought out between two champions, I representing the poorer boys who lived in flats and my opponent the richer boys who lived in the opposite villas. We fought in the garden of one of the said villas and had an excellent contest of many rounds, not being strong enough to weaken each other. When I got home after the battle, my mother cried, "Oh, Arthur, what a dreadful eye you have got!" To which I replied, "You just go across and look at Eddie Tulloch's eye"!'

It was a hard, traditionally working-class, Scottish inner-city childhood. And Conan Doyle's mother was shocked by it all. She had not expected this for her son; nor expected it for herself either. But one thing Mary could do for her boy was to encourage him to read. Initially she had to force him to look at his books but before long it was almost as difficult to stop him reading and get him to eat his meals and go to bed. It was a perennial factor in Conan Doyle's life that he was always aware of and instinctively perceived the meeting-point between body and mind, between the physical and the intellectual. There was no division, no dichotomy, no contradiction for him between reading about romantic battles and chivalric deeds and then fighting for individual honour, for the tribe or just for the block of flats in which he lived. More than this, it seemed to him that the two aspects of life were the opposite of being mutually exclusive and were, to a very large extent, mutually essential if both were to be understood. What Conan Doyle read about in tales of adventure only achieved full meaning if he could in some way or other act them out in his own life – schoolboy fights when he was young, battlefield heroics when he grew to maturity. He never understood, and never liked, those people who regarded themselves as intellectuals with a limited concern for the body. They simply did not understand, he said.

He devoured books; held them close, read and reread favourite lines and passages, searched for more, borrowed, asked for advice for further reading. They were a passion. The library was helpful but insufficient because it refused to exchange books more than twice a day. 'I wrote a little book and illustrated it myself in early days,' he recorded in his memoirs. 'There was a man in it and there was a tiger who amalgamated shortly after they met. I remarked to my mother with precocious wisdom that it was easy to get people into scrapes, but not so easy to get them out again, which is surely the experience of every writer of adventures.'

Conan Doyle left his hated Edinburgh school when his mother – who was increasingly the driving force in the home – decided that the boy's Roman Catholic education had to be expanded and supervised. Mary's passionate belief in what she thought was her authentic social standing and her strict adherence to her religion meant that there were only two schools possible for her son, Downside, where the Benedictines taught, and Stonyhurst College, where the Jesuits imposed their own particular brand of education on their pupils. The family decided on the latter and Conan Doyle was sent down to Lancashire, to Stonyhurst's preparatory school, Hodder, only a mile or so away from the main school.

Conan Doyle began at Hodder in 1868 as he approached his tenth birthday, and on his first day at the school he cried all morning. But his two years were relatively good ones for the little boy, who was fortunate enough to be taken under the wing of a fair-minded, gentle and tolerant master by the name of Father Cassidy – 'more human than Jesuits usually are' Conan Doyle later remarked – and he got on well with the other boys. The Jesuits had already approached Charles and Mary and offered an arrangement whereby, in exchange for young Arthur being given over to the Church, his vocation apparently guaranteed, the annual fee of £50 would be waived. This would save a fifth of Charles's income but he still decided that his son was too young to be packed off to a life that might not be at all suitable for him. It was something for which his son would always be grateful.

The school that Conan Doyle entered in 1870 was a 'grand medieval dwelling-house which was left some hundred and fifty years ago to the Jesuits, who brought over their whole teaching staff from some college in Holland in order to carry it on as a public school,' wrote Conan Doyle.[4] 'The general curriculum, like the building, was medieval but sound . . . There were seven classes – elements, figures, rudiments, grammar, syntax, poetry and rhetoric – and you were allotted a year for each, or seven in all – a course with which I faithfully complied, two having already been completed at Hodder. It was the usual public school routine of Euclid, algebra and the classics, taught in the usual way, which is calculated to leave a lasting abhorrence of these subjects. To give boys a little slab of Virgil or Homer with no general idea as to what it is all about or what the classical age was like, is surely an absurd way of treating the subject.'

He thought the same about the Jesuits' way of teaching Roman Catholicism. He had never been an especially religious boy despite or perhaps because of, his mother's faithfulness, but he did have an interest in belief and faith. Any reservations or indifference he possessed before he went to Stonyhurst was hardened into something approaching hostility under the guiding hands of the Jesuits. In their defence, the regime they imposed on the boys was not much different from that of the non-Catholic public schools in Britain at the time. Stonyhurst had opened in 1794, the result of the Napoleonic wars, a fact Conan Doyle remembered when he came to write his historical romances based on the era. By the second half of the nineteenth century, partly as a result of the massive waves of Irish immigration, many of Conan Doyle's young contemporaries were Irish or of predominantly Irish descent. They, like the school, felt that they had something to prove and a standard to set themselves.

There were fewer than 300 students at Stonyhurst in 1870, all of them initiated into the esoteric rituals of the college with its rooms with names such as Washing Place, Strangers' Place and Shoe Place. The education was thorough, the teaching exact, but the flavour and style of Stonyhurst was based on fear and intimidation rather than loyalty and respect. The Jesuit masters did not even try to teach and convince the boys by compassion or warmth – perhaps they had not even been shown how – but instead used the threat of violent corporal punishment and ritual humiliation. They used prefects who were no better than spies or informers to keep the other boys in order and had an obsessive fear of the boys indulging in masturbation or acts of homosexuality. This made the boys, and certainly Conan Doyle, even more self-conscious than they otherwise would have been.

One of the punishments peculiar to Stonyhurst was something known as the 'penance-walk', where a boy was forced to walk on his own, in complete silence, around the playground for an hour with other boys looking on and sometimes taunting him. Most of the beatings were administered by specially chosen masters with something resembling the sole of a slipper called a 'ferula' and known by the pupils as a 'tolly'. Masters were allowed to hit the boys nine times on each hand if they had been particularly disobedient or difficult. The result would be swelling and discoloration and it could take weeks for the wounds inflicted to disappear and heal.

The birch was also allowed and Conan Doyle was beaten more than almost any other boy at Stonyhurst. Yet he appeared to bear no grudge. On the contrary, he later wrote: 'I think, however, that it was good for us in the end, for it was a point of honour with many of us not to show that we were hurt, and that is one of the best trainings for a hard life. If I was more beaten than others it was not that I was in any way vicious, but it was that I had a nature which responded eagerly to affectionate kindness (which I never received), but which rebelled against threats and took a perverted pride in showing that it would not be cowed by violence. I went out of my way to do really mischievous and outrageous things simply to show that my spirit was unbroken. An appeal to my better nature and not to my fears would have found an answer at once. I deserved all I got for what I did, but I did it because I was mishandled.'

If the punishment was severe, the food and drink were worse, apart from on Fridays, when some of the fish dishes, especially the fish pie, were quite appetizing. The standard fare was dry bread and hot milk, supplemented in the winter by thick porridge and a stew with potatoes that the boys detested but which filled their bellies and gave them sufficient energy for the school's sports programme. In addition to the usual English sports the boys also played some games imported from Holland. 'Cat' and 'Trap' were two of these, the former being a variation on rounders. Conan Doyle excelled at both. Football was popular and cricket was a favourite sport, although it too had its own oddities at Stonyhurst, such as a stone instead of a wicket. One of the main reasons for these variants was that whatever Stonyhurst was or tried to be, it was not a Protestant school. It knew it, and other schools knew it as well. Church of England public schools were as reluctant to play Stonyhurst at sports as Stonyhurst was loath to play them. Two unsplendid isolations, twin solitudes of ignorance. The shame of this for Conan Doyle was that he could have reached the highest levels in both cricket and football if he had been allowed to improve his performance by competing against other schools and other, more able boys.

He was a natural athlete and a naturally large and powerful youth. By his fifteenth birthday he was five feet nine inches tall and was just on the right side of plumpness. In fact he was more the athlete than the scholar and disappointed the masters and his parents with his lack of academic success. 'One master, when I told him that I thought of being a civil engineer, remarked, "Well, Doyle, you may be an engineer, but I don't think you will ever be a civil one." Another assured me that I would never do any good in the world, and perhaps from his point of view his prophecy has been justified.' What this apparent failure and genuine condemnation did manage to provoke was a passion for private study and for writing – there was nobody to criticize him when he was alone with a book. Even though he was a very modest man he did record in latter life that at school he realized that 'I had some literary streak in me which was not common to all'.

One of the people who developed this leaning, perhaps unwittingly, was Conan Doyle's uncle Richard, of *Punch* fame, who took his nephew to see several plays in London, including *Hamlet* with Henry Irving and *Our American Cousin* at the Haymarket Theatre. Conan Doyle was startled by the possibilities of the written word, liberated from the greyness of his days at Stonyhurst, where literature seldom jumped from the page, principally because it was not allowed to do so. He began to read Macaulay and Sir Walter Scott, to reread some of the military and more gory chapters of his Bible and to write to his relatives asking for the latest magazines and some of their favourite novels. He was also experimenting with his writing, trying out characters and plots but, regrettably, rarely keeping his notes and journals. In his last year at Stonyhurst he was asked to edit the school magazine, which he did with his usual enthusiasm and energy. Those young writers who worked for him remembered him as being demanding but understanding. He was to adopt a similar attitude towards others for most of his life.

In 1875 he was sent by the Jesuits to another of their schools, at Feldkirch in Austria, to learn German. 'Here the conditions were much more humane and I met with far more human kindness than at Stonyhurst, with the immediate result that I ceased to be a resentful young rebel and became a pillar of law and order. I began badly, however, for on the first night of my arrival I was kept awake by a boy snoring loudly in the dormitory. I stood it as long as I could, but at last I was driven to action. Curious wooden compasses called bett-scheere, or "bed-scissors", were stuck into each side of the narrow beds. One of these I plucked out, walked down the dormitory, and, having spotted the offender, proceeded to poke him with my stick. He awoke and was considerably amazed to see in the dim light a large youth whom he had never seen before – I arrived after hours – assaulting him with a club. I was still engaged in stirring him up when I felt a touch on my shoulder and was confronted by the master, who ordered me back to bed. Next morning I got a lecture on free-and-easy English ways, and taking the law into my own hands. But this start was really my worst lapse and I did well in the future.'

He did well and he enjoyed himself. There was snow here and he was taught how to toboggan properly and mastered the rudiments of other winter sports. He played football, wrestled and received tuition in the bombardon, a form of valved bass tuba, something he would joke about later. All in all this inexperienced Scottish boy with a devoted mother and weak father, who had been sent off at an early age to be taught by often cruel priests, had matured by the time he was sixteen into a remarkably well-adjusted and mature young man. He was robust and intelligent, wise for his years and regarded by others as a loyal friend. He was also a natural leader, good in a crisis and frequently nominated by other boys as their spokesman and leader. With women and girls he was less adept, having met very few socially and behaving awkwardly with them when he did make contact. There was never any suggestion of homosexuality attaching to Conan Doyle, either as a young man or an adult – at least not in the physical sense. He did, however, form close personal ties and friendships with men later on in his life. The only student at Stonyhurst with whom he remained close friends was a boy named James Ryan. These were not the happiest days of his life, in spite of what people insisted on telling him.

After completing his studies in Feldkirch Conan Doyle left for home and broke his journey in Paris to visit the great uncle after whom he was named but had never actually met. He had spent most of his allowance in Austria and lavished almost all of what remained on a grand supper in Strasburg. Reluctant to arrive at his uncle's door with an unpaid cab driver at his back, he left his trunk at the station in Paris and walked to his uncle's house. 'So, for some penurious weeks, I was in Paris with this dear old volcanic Irishman, who spent the summer day in his shirt-sleeves, with a little dicky-bird of a wife waiting upon him. I am built rather on his lines of body and mind than on any of the Doyles. We made a true friendship,' he wrote. Michael Conan was a deep thinker, a man, regrettably, whose thoughts were far greater and far more profound than his deeds. His stories of travel and adventure inspired Conan Doyle and he never forgot this short but important hiatus in his life between Austria and Scotland.

Back in Britain and in possession of some German grammar and vocabulary, and with some travel and experience under his belt – one that occasionally had to be loosened because of a life-long tendency to gain weight even though he constantly exercised – Conan Doyle, it was decided, would go to Edinburgh University and study to become a doctor. Edinburgh was chosen because the family could not have afforded Oxford or Cambridge; could not have afforded any university in England for that matter. Nor was this an orthodox university, as is Edinburgh University today. Nobody lived in or at the university, there were no colleges as such and no time to enjoy the extracurricular activities available to students in England or those with more money and resources. Students went to Edinburgh for no other reason than to learn and to qualify and if they failed their exams they had, effectively, wasted their money, which they paid directly to their teachers.

Charles and Mary Doyle's decision to send their son off to study medicine was an easy one because the medical profession possessed a straightforward and solid structure; once qualified as a doctor Conan Doyle could make a living. Philosophy and literature were all very well but bread and butter and a full stomach were even better. This was the family's view and Conan Doyle, ever the realist in such matters, concurred. Edinburgh had a good reputation for medicine, its lecturers were known to be progressive and competent and, best of all, it was walking distance from home.

Money was still short, even with Conan Doyle's sister Annette sending money back from Portugal and another two about to become wage-earners. He was always an honourable man, usually a proud one, and applied for virtually every scholarship open to him. Having managed to win one of them, worth £20 a year, he was astounded to realize after the results were announced that he had made an error and that the scholarship was in fact available only to arts students. After attempts at gaining several other grants he ended up winning only one, for just £7, and as a consequence was obliged to take outside paid work. He was even forced to work, throughout his student days, as an assistant to a doctor. In reality he was working as a doctor himself; ironically, he had to work in medicine before he had completed his medical studies in order to pay for the rest of the course. This might have proved worrying, particularly for his patients, but he seems to have done quite well at the work. He spent time in Sheffield with a Dr Richardson in the summer of 1878, in Shropshire with Dr Elliot and later in Birmingham with Dr Hoare. He returned to the Birmingham work, both because it paid better than others and because it enabled him to see some of the poorer and more criminally inclined inhabitants of the inner city and to gain an experience of the seedier side of life. Much of Sherlock Holmes's London is in fact the Edinburgh of the child Conan Doyle, and the Birmingham of the nineteen-year-old student.

This was a great deal of hard work; nor was he always satisfied with the education he was receiving. He was at times extremely disappointed with the university and wondered what he was doing there. He summed up his university career thus: 'I entered as a student in October 1876, and I emerged as a Bachelor of Medicine in August 1881. Between these two points lies one long weary grind at botany, chemistry, anatomy, physiology, and a whole list of compulsory subjects, many of which have a very indirect bearing upon the art of curing.' In the years that Conan Doyle studied at Edinburgh the student population in the faculty of medicine grew rapidly, rising from 1000 at the beginning of his studies to over 1500 by the time he left. With the increased number of students came an enlargement of facilities, including a club for the students and the organization of sporting events. And there was now more going on than merely the chatter of the bland teachers and the indifferent professors. There were some remarkable and amusing young men coming to Edinburgh.

'There was kindly Crum Brown, the chemist, who sheltered himself carefully before exploding some mixture, which usually failed to ignite, so that the loud "Boom!" uttered by the class was the only resulting sound. Brown would emerge from his retreat with a "Really, gentlemen!" of remonstrance, and go on without allusion to the abortive experiment. There was Wyville Thomson, the zoologist, fresh from his Challenger expedition, and Balfour, with the face and manner of John Knox, a hard rugged man, who harried students in their exams, and was in consequence harried by them for the rest of the year. There was Turner, a fine anatomist, but a self-educated man, as was betrayed when he used to "take and put this structure on the handle of this scalpel". The most human trait that I can recall of

Turner was that upon one occasion the sacred quadrangle was invaded by snowballing roughs. His class, of whom I was one, heard the sounds of battle and fidgeted in their seats, on which the professor said: "I think, gentlemen, your presence may be more useful outside than here", on which we flocked out with a whoop, and soon had the quadrangle clear.'[5]

Each of these men would reappear in Conan Doyle's fiction, principally in the Sherlock Holmes stories, and Conan Doyle himself once told G.K. Chesterton that no writer ever needed to go any further than a classroom, assembly hall or police station to find enough characters to fill any number of novels.[6] But there was perhaps one man who would not have been found so readily in any ordinary surroundings. Dr Joseph Bell made a lasting impression on most of his students, but particularly on Conan Doyle. His physical appearance was striking, being a combination of a dark, almost saturnine complexion, grey, piercing eyes, a long, thin and wiry body with angular shoulders and limbs and a strange, jerky way of walking. The voice which emanated from this strange-looking man was surprisingly high-pitched and demanded attention. His reputation at the university was that of a Renaissance man, skilled not only as a teacher but as a poet, cricketer, boxer and tennis player, with an interest in nature, dialects and handwriting and an ability to shoot, ice-skate and discourse on the finer points of ornithology. He was known to read Scott, Carlyle, Browning and the Bible, to be fascinated by military history and police affairs, to have an erratic but strong sense of humour and to possess the ability to divine an enormous amount of information about his students and patients by unconventional and surprising means. Simply, a fascinating and charismatic figure who would change Conan Doyle's life and, through him, the lives of many others.

'For some reason which I have never understood he singled me out from the drove of students who frequented his wards and made me his out-patient clerk, which meant that

I had to array his out-patients, make simple notes of their cases, and then show them in, one by one, to the large room in which Bell sat in state surrounded by his dressers and students. Then I had ample chance of studying his methods and of noticing that he often learned more of the patient by a few quick glances than I had done by my questions. Occasionally the results were very dramatic, though there were times when he blundered. In one of his best cases he said to a civilian patient: "Well, my man, you've served in the army."

"Aye, sir."

"Not long discharged?"

"No, sir."

"A Highland regiment?"

"Aye, sir."

"A non-com officer?"

"Aye, sir."

"Stationed at Barbados?"

"Aye, sir."

"You see, gentlemen," he would explain, "the man was a respectful man but did not remove his hat. They do not in the army, but he would have learned civilian ways had he been long discharged. He has an air of authority and he is obviously Scottish. As to Barbados, his complaint is elephantiasis, which is West Indian and not British."' To his audience of Watsons it all seemed very miraculous until it was explained, and then it became simple and easy enough. 'It is no wonder that after the study of such a character I used and amplified his methods when in later life I tried to build up a scientific detective who solved cases on his own merits and not through the folly of the criminal. Bell took a keen interest in these detective tales and even made suggestions which were not, I am bound to say, very practical.'

If major aspects of a future detective were to be found in Joseph Bell, another man whom Conan Doyle met at Edinburgh who would influence his writing was the anatomist Professor John Rutherford. This eccentric, electric figure, with his impressive dark beard and bellowing voice, did not make the same impression as his colleague Bell but he too would be transformed into a fictional character, this time more than three decades later and under the name of Professor Challenger.

Events in Conan Doyle's private life were lending him a degree of maturity and determining his future direction. Among them was the fact that in 1879 his father entered a nursing home for the first of several stays. Charles Doyle had shown signs of mental instability for the past two years, had spent entire days and nights in bed and drank not for pleasure but to escape a life with which he was increasingly unhappy. He was an alcoholic and an epileptic. He disliked Scotland, disliked Roman Catholicism, and disliked his relative failure. Everyone around him seemed to be achieving things, fulfilling their potential. Were they speaking about him behind his back, making fun of his lack of success? He became unloving towards his wife and indifferent towards his children. Mary finally announced that she could not cope with her husband and that he would have to be cared for professionally. The family broke up and Mary went to live in Yorkshire, in Masongill Cottage on the Waller estate. Her eldest son assumed the role of the late-Victorian man of the house in Edinburgh. He was not yet twenty years old.

At the beginning of 1880 Conan Doyle made a typically astounding decision, probably influenced by distress at his father's breakdown. This steadfast young man decided to interrupt his studies and sign on as a surgeon on board a whaling ship, the *Hope*, which would sail from Peterhead to the Arctic. The voyage would offer any amount of adventure, as well as its fair share of opportunities to be killed or badly injured. One of Conan Doyle's friends had originally been given the post but he had been forced to withdraw at the last moment. Would Conan Doyle replace him? How could he not? It was an opportunity to spend seven months on a ship with a crew of fifty, seeing corners of the world that he might not otherwise ever come close to, meeting hardened sailors who had any number of anecdotes to tell. Some of his friends and relatives advised against it, warning that no aspiring gentleman went off on a working ship for the best part of a year and that no sane man would risk his well-being for anything less than a fortune. Conan Doyle accepted the position almost immediately.

The trip did him nothing but good. He enjoyed, and would then always enjoy, the company of working men, of people he regarded as earthy and realistic. For Conan Doyle the flavour of the extraordinary was to be captured within the taste of the most ordinary. In his life and his writing he perceived the most beguiling and colourful scenes and people in places and in individuals who were, to some observers, ostensibly banal and commonplace. Perhaps they were the latter, but this made them all the more exciting and vibrant for their young doctor. The tough, no-nonsense men with whom he shared his life for seven months were natural storytellers, sitting Conan Doyle down and telling him of their lives. There could be no better training school for a developing writer. He devotes several pages to the trip in his autobiography, explaining the background and character of several of the Scottish and Shetland men on the ship, and he takes special pleasure in writing about the region and its isolation.

'Your sense of loneliness also heightens the effect of the Arctic seas. When we were in whaling latitudes it is probable that, with the exception of our consort, there was no vessel within 800 miles of us. For seven long months no letter and no news came to us from the southern world. We had left in exciting times. The Afghan campaign had been undertaken, and war seemed imminent with Russia. We returned opposite the mouth of the Baltic without any means of knowing whether some cruiser might not treat us as we had treated the whales. When we met a fishing-boat at the north of Shetland our first inquiry was as to peace or war. Great events had happened during those seven months:

the defeat of Maiwand and the famous march of Roberts from Cabul to Candahar. But it was all haze to us; and, to this day, I have never been able to get that particular bit of military history straightened out in my own mind.

'The perpetual light, the glare of the white ice, the deep blue of the water, these are the things which one remembers most clearly, and the dry, crisp, exhilarating air, which makes mere life the keenest of pleasures. And then there are the innumerable sea-birds, whose call is for ever ringing in your ears – the gulls, the fulmars, the snow-birds, the burgomasters, the looms, and the rotjes. These fill the air, and below, the waters are for ever giving you a peep of some strange new creature. The commercial whale may not often come your way, but his less valuable brethren abound on every side . . . I went on board the whaler a big, straggling youth, I came off it a powerful, well-grown man. I have no doubt that my physical health during my whole life has been affected by that splendid air, and that the inexhaustible store of energy which I have enjoyed is to some extent drank from the same source.'[7]

It is also significant that he had been writing steadily in his spare time, composing adventure stories and historical romances. Most of these were for his own enjoyment but he realized, and was told by his friends, that no writer is satisfied with only writing for himself. He must publish. He was reluctant, however, and at first sent out the stories to magazines with a request that his name not be used. He had surprisingly little difficulty in getting his early work accepted. In October 1879 *Chambers' Journal* printed his story 'The Mystery of Sarassa Valley', a tale heavily influenced by an African legend about a demon with fierce eyes who terrified local villagers. Conan Doyle was paid three guineas for the piece. Shortly afterwards the magazine *London Society* bought and published 'The American's Tale'. He was astounded and delighted. Serious editors, serious people, were giving him money for his words, paying him for pouring out on paper the thoughts in his head.

For the first time since beginning his medical studies he thought that he might just carve out a career as something other than a doctor. But he pushed these ambitions to the back of his mind, aware that he couldn't yet survive on his income as a writer.

Most important of all, this period at the end of the 1870s and early 1880s saw the development of Conan Doyle's spiritual self. He questioned and finally rejected the Roman Catholic interpretation of Christianity, indeed the whole nineteenth-century version of the Christian story. Yet if contemporary Christianity was unsatisfying and invalid it did not mean that there was not some greater force working in the world. To paraphrase G.K. Chesterton, when some men stop believing in something they do not then believe in nothing, they believe in everything. Conan Doyle could never believe in nothing; it was not in his character. But he longed all of his life to believe, in both a secular and temporal way. Country, flag, empire, family, honour, religion. The last was central. So if the Church was to be abandoned he had to look to an alternative. As he himself said, he was 'driven to agnosticism, which never for an instant degenerated into atheism, for I had a very keen perception of the wonderful poise of the universe and the tremendous power of conception and sustenance which it implied'.

He described himself as a Unitarian at this stage in his life but later on and with the advantage of hindsight he realized that this was no more than a convenient halfway house. The charm, beauty and seductive ritual of Catholicism had not quite let him go. He had abandoned the substantial but not the cosmetic aspects of his baptismal faith. What he began to believe was that life on earth was only one visible, tangible manifestation of a greater, broader, longer existence and that death was merely a passage, a conduit to something far greater. In a letter he wrote later during a debate over Roman Catholicism he explained that he was already 'a believer in something I later identified as spiritualism' when he worked on board the *Hope*.[8] He states that several of the men, particularly those from the Scottish islands, claimed to have had spiritual experiences both at home and while at sea. Most of these men were, apparently, from breakaway Presbyterian churches in which the drinking of alcohol was forbidden. They were not drunk when they had their visions. Conan Doyle may have been young but he was not overly credulous and not really naive. He questioned them on their state of mind at the time of their visions, on their broader attitudes and so on. He also wondered if they were making fun of him. It all seemed quite genuine and Conan Doyle was convinced that there was something in what the men had to say. When he returned to Scotland he was definitely embarking on his spiritualist journey and was in the early stages of adopting an organized religious belief.

Once back in Edinburgh he accepted his medical degree, visited his friends and family and then, without wasting too much time thinking about establishing a career, he signed up for another voyage at sea, this time as surgeon on board a 4000-ton cargo ship called the SS *Mayumba*, carrying thirty passengers, most of whom were travelling to Madeira. He was to be paid £12 a month. The ship left Liverpool on 22 October 1881. Conan Doyle was more seasick on this trip than he had been on the one to the Arctic and quickly realized one of the major disadvantages of being a doctor on a ship in troubled water: when the passengers were sick, so was he, yet he was being paid to look after *them*. It was not a pleasant experience. Later in the voyage, however, the seas quietened, the weather grew hotter and everybody and everything calmed down.

The men on the whaler had been more entertaining for Conan Doyle than his new crew and it was only when the *Mayumba* docked at various destinations that he enjoyed his time. They reached Freetown, the capital of Sierra Leone, on 9 November. Conan Doyle described it as a beautiful spot but a place of death. 'It was a truly dreadful place in the early eighties, and the despair which reigned in the hearts of the white people made them take liberties with alcohol which they would not have dared to take in a healthier place. A year's residence seemed to be about the limit of human endurance. I remember meeting one healthy-looking resident who told me that he had been there three years. When I congratulated him he shook his head. "I am a doomed man. I have advanced Bright's disease," said he. One wondered whether the colonies were really worth the price we had to pay.'

From Sierra Leone Conan Doyle's ship travelled to Liberia, the country founded by freed or escaped American slaves. He was amused by the self-importance of the tiny country, which during the Franco-German war sent out its only Customs boat to represent its navy and inform the European powers that Liberia would not be interfering in the conflict. He spent three days with the United States Minister to Liberia and with the black abolitionist leader Henry Highland Garnet. Much of the scenery of the region, whether it was Liberia, the Ivory Coast or the Gold Coast, appeared the same to this now quite experienced traveller and he thought it vapid and dull. It could also be dangerous, and this was something that Conan Doyle appreciated. He hunted for alligators, swam in shark-infested waters with the locals and hiked through jungles inhabited by poisonous insects and carnivorous creatures. He escaped being eaten or bitten by a snake but by the time he reached Lagos on 18 November he was suffering from a potentially fatal fever, probably malarial, carried by the mosquitoes. He recalled the attack in some memorable prose: 'I remember staggering to my bunk and then all was blotted out. As I was myself doctor there was no one to look after me and I lay for several days fighting it out with Death in a very small ring and without a second. It speaks well for my constitution that I came out a victor. I remember no psychic experience, no vision, no fears, nothing save a nightmare fog from which I emerged as weak as a child. It must have been a close call, and I had scarcely sat up before I heard that another victim who got it at the same time was dead.'

He moved on, up the River Bonny, where he saw natives who offered up human sacrifices to the sharks. His captain had heard the screams of the victims as they were dragged towards the water and seen a skull of one poor wretch protruding from an anthill. He met missionaries, who he thought might not have converted the aboriginals but had certainly helped to civilize them. His uncertain attitude was indicative of his general enlightenment on the issue of race. Of course Conan Doyle was a Victorian with the general attitudes of the era, but his support for the proselytizers was motivated more by sympathy for the plight of so many of the Africans than concern for their immortal souls. If we bear in mind that he was only twenty-two when he travelled around Africa we realize just how determined and mature this young man was. Most grand tours consisted of visiting picturesque European cities. Conan Doyle had been told at school to write about what he knew; his range of topics was expanding exponentially. 'Getting a canoe, I ascended the river for several miles to a place called Creektown. Dark and terrible mangrove swamps lay on either side with gloomy shades where nothing that is not horrible could exist. It is indeed a foul place. Once in an isolated tree, standing in a flood, I saw an evil-looking snake, worm-coloured and about 3 feet long. I shot him and saw him drift down stream. I learned later in life to give up killing animals, but I confess that I have no particular compunctions about that one.'⁹

If he later made the decision not to slaughter animals he certainly had amends to make from his earlier days. From his own writings and from what he told his friends it is clear that he shot almost everything of any size or anything that could in any way be considered a threat. There was a yard-long fish that swam to the surface near his ship. He fired at it and killed the poor creature. Within seconds another fish appeared, seized the corpse by its middle and dragged it beneath the water to devour it. Conan Doyle was shocked by this – 'so murderous is the food-search, and so keen the watch of Nature!' – but continued to cradle his gun as he sailed through and around the continent. 'The death-like impression of Africa grew upon me,' he wrote. 'One felt that the white man with his present diet and habits was an intruder who was never meant to be there, and that the great sullen brown continent killed him as one crushes nits.'

By mid-January 1882 Conan Doyle was back in Liverpool. Strengthened by his time in Africa, and tinged by the cruelty he had seen, he made the momentous decision to announce to the world, or at least to his mother, that he had completely abandoned his Roman Catholicism. It shows how close the relationship between the mother and son was that this convinced and orthodox Catholic woman accepted his statement without argument. Later on in her life she abandoned Catholicism as well, under the influence if not the pressure of her son. He also told her of his time in Africa, of what he had seen and felt and asked her for advice about his career. It was not that he particularly wanted maternal help in deciding his future; more that he knew she was terribly isolated without her husband and at times felt useless and redundant. There was a bond between mother and son that was more empathetic and sensitive than most such relationships and there was also a genuine mutual respect. Ironically, and gloriously, it made Conan Doyle the independent young man he was by 1882. And it gave him the confidence and maturity to realize that it was time to settle down to a profession that would, he assumed, sustain and satisfy him for the rest of his life. He was, after all, a doctor.

2

Doctoring and Detection

The young doctor was well seasoned for his age. He looked older than his twenty-two years, with his thick, dark moustache extending from high on his upper lip to below the top of his teeth, his hooded eyes and his round, plump face. He combed his hair across his forehead in long waves, firming it down with oils. He was broad, weighed fifteen stone when in shape and was inclined to be heavier, with a forceful manner and a walk that others said always made him look as though he knew exactly where he was going and was determined to get there, no matter what stood in his way. He laughed at good jokes, pretended to laugh at bad ones. He drank beer and wine and enjoyed Scotch when he wasn't working. He insisted on three meals a day and had the habit of waking in the middle of the night to read or write while eating bread and cheese and drinking warmed beer. His Edinburgh accent was strong but his speech was fairly slow so that he was easily understood. When he spoke to someone he came close to them, touched their arm, looked into their eyes, was personable, apparently always interested. Some said he would make a fine politician, but others said he was far too genuine and honest for that. Others still thought that he wouldn't remain a doctor all of his life.

Conan Doyle needed security and security seemed to be

offered, from the wild west. He had known a Dr George Turnavine Budd in Edinburgh for some years and this eccentric, notoriously unreliable and formerly bankrupt man now and without warning sent a telegram from Plymouth announcing that he had become an enormous success and that Conan Doyle should come at once if he knew what was good for him. Conan Doyle was urged by his mother to write back with some questions about details and figures. So confident was Budd that he replied with another telegram, this time angry: 'Your letter to hand. Why not call me a liar at once? I tell you that I have seen thirty thousand patients in the last year. My actual takings have been more than four thousand pounds. All patients come to me. We would not cross the street to see Queen Victoria. You can have all visiting, all surgery, all midwifery. Will guarantee three hundred pounds the first year.' It all seemed to be too good to be true. It turned out that it was neither good nor true.

Budd was not only mercurial and boastful, but he was also often malicious towards his patients and invariably uncaring towards his friends. He exploited the poor of Plymouth, gave them drugs that had no effect and might even have been harmful and led them on with lies about their complaints, frightening them into coming to see him for months when there was no real cause. But Conan Doyle found this new offer irresistible; if he had risked Arctic whales and African sharks he could surely survive Plymouth's worst dangers. At first he was eager to believe everything he was told by his new partner, who had apparently been so generous with his good fortune. But such credulity was difficult to maintain. Budd was alternately callous and affectionate and would suddenly indulge in absurd behaviour such as parading his daily earnings in front of his patients, partly to humiliate them but mostly just for the effect and the shock of it. He was probably half-mad. Conan Doyle chronicled his time in Plymouth in his book *The Stark Munro Letters*, an almost completely autobiographical work which reveals Dr Budd as a profoundly strange and difficult man. In his memoirs Conan Doyle wrote of an incident where 'dropsy had disappeared before a severe dose of croton oil in a way that set all the gossips talking. People flocked into the town from 20 and 30 miles round, and not only his waiting-rooms, but his stairs and his passages were crammed. His behaviour to them was extraordinary. He roared and shouted, scolded them, joked them, pushed them about, and pursued them sometimes into the street, or addressed them collectively from the landing. A morning with him when the practice was in full blast was as funny as any pantomime and I was exhausted with laughter. He had a well-worn volume on Medical Jurisprudence which he pretended was the Bible, and he swore old women on it that they would drink no more tea.'

As time wore on Conan Doyle found Dr Budd less amusing and more worrying. He wrote to his mother to tell her about his colleague and the woman returned wise letters advising him to end the partnership. She also told her son in no uncertain terms what she thought of this man with whom he was in partnership. Unbeknown to Conan Doyle, an especially vitriolic letter from Mary fell into Budd's hands and the man flew into one of his accustomed rages. He demanded that Conan Doyle leave the surgery and set up on his own, disguising his motives by explaining that the locals wanted only one doctor, one with whom they were comfortable, and that Conan Doyle was redundant and even damaging to the practice. It would be best if Conan Doyle left, for everyone's sake. In reaction the young doctor ripped his brass name-plate from the door of the Plymouth house with a hammer and screwdriver and threatened dire consequences. But Budd then seemed to soften and announced that he would give his friend a pound a week if he left the town and tried to find work elsewhere, adding that this would surely be the best solution for both of them.

As he calmed down Conan Doyle began to realize that he would be best advised to get out while he could and take the offer while it was still open. He decided to move to Portsmouth. In the event the offer of the weekly pound did not last very long; Budd wrote to the twenty-three-year-old explaining that he had found Mary Doyle's letter and was extremely angry. There would be no more money. With only around £10 to his name Conan Doyle was going to find a life of independent doctoring rather a problem. Mary went to her personal savings, not a grand amount, and gave her son all the money she could.

Conan Doyle arrived in Portsmouth and immediately rented a house with the grandiloquent name of Bush Villa in the residential suburb of Southsea for £40 a year. 'I had obtained a fair consignment of drugs on tick from a wholesale house and these also were ranged round the sides of the back room. From the very beginning a few stray patients of the poorest class, some of them desirous of novelty, some disgruntled with their own doctors, the greater part owing bills and ashamed to face their creditor, came to consult me and consume a bottle of my medicine. I could pay for my food by the drugs I sold. It was as well, for I had no other way of paying for it, and I had sworn not to touch the ten golden pieces which represented my rent. There have been times when I could not buy a postage stamp and my letters have had to wait, but the ten golden coins still remained intact.'

The expected stream of patients simply did not materialize and Conan Doyle had not anticipated the intensity of competition from other doctors in the area. Nor would he exploit those patients who did come to see him, unlike his former partner in Plymouth. He had always been a man of integrity and financial hardship was not going to change that. But there was no denying that things were very bad. He lost more than fifteen pounds in weight and was frequently hungry. This made him weak, which in turn made him depressed. In a rather pathetic example of primitive bartering he was given butter, milk and tea by an epileptic grocer who needed regular medical treatment during his fits and afterwards when he was in recovery. He was forced to pawn his watch and to wear fraying clothes that earlier in his life he would have discarded.

But still he liked Southsea, relishing its intimacy with history and empire, with the Royal Navy's exploits and with the writings of Charles Dickens. He always said in later life that it was his favourite town. And things did improve, to such an extent that at one point he was able to hire a housekeeper to help with the cooking and cleaning and give him some feeling of professional autonomy. It was a needless expense and one he couldn't really afford. Another financial drain was more of an investment, or at least appeared to be. He joined various sports clubs in central Portsmouth and Southsea, playing football, trying his hand at bowling and becoming captain of Portsmouth cricket club. One of the intentions here was to meet a far wider circle of people and increase his list of patients and in this he succeeded. He began to see not only more but more wealthy people at his surgery. The sports clubs, and some debating circles that he also joined, were composed of the rising middle class. Just the sort of people, his mother wrote to him, that he should be helping and befriending.

Sport was essential to Conan Doyle, and he would probably have joined the clubs whether it helped his work or not. Up until the final years of his life he was the most extraordinarily robust of men, with so much energy that if he did not exercise in the day he could not sleep at night. Walking, running or playing sport was no more a recreation for him than eating or drinking. It was a necessity. He would pace around a room like a caged animal, run upstairs and tap his feet incessantly if he could not get out for a fast walk or a jog. When he played football he made up for his lack of natural skill with a determination that astounded other players. He was usually a defender but would sprint to the opponent's goal whenever he could, seldom receiving the ball, and then run back to his own position again to repel a counter-attack. Constant movement, running and alertness were the order of the day. Spectators referred to him as a coiled spring of a man.

This description also applied to his intellectual side. He read quickly and indiscriminately. There were some books in the study of the house he had rented and he read them all, whatever they were. Then he went through all of Gibbon, returned to his beloved Carlyle and spent many evenings at the Portsmouth Literary and Scientific Society lecturing on his favourite authors. He would read through reference books for hours on end simply for pleasure. He was writing too, and had a story entitled 'Habakuk Jephson's Statement', based on the *Marie Celeste* mystery, published in the highly regarded *Cornhill Magazine*. They paid him the munificent fee of twenty-nine guineas. He and his mother found it hard to believe. He also began a novel, *The Firm of Girdlestone*, about his days at university, which would eventually be published in 1890. And there were some essays and stories published in *Boy's Own Paper* and *All the Year Round*.

One novel, *The Narrative of John Smith*, was tragically lost in the mail and other works were rejected by publishers and magazine editors. Indeed the *Cornhill Magazine* turned down several pieces after 'Habakuk Jephson's Statement'. But Conan Doyle wasn't downhearted, or at least not enough to give up this lucrative side career. He was also writing letters to the local press and to national medical journals. He had already had a letter published in the *Lancet* of March 1882 about a case of leucocythaemia he had seen and wrote another to the *Medical Times* in June 1883 about the Contagious Diseases Act. To the *Evening News* in Portsmouth he wrote about the Young Men's Christian Association and a dispute about its name. He launched into an attack on a censorious clergyman, ending his letter by arguing that if this clergyman's definition of Christianity were accepted 'one would have to choose between Mohametanism and Atheism'.[1]

This was the sort of writing he enjoyed – varied and all – embracing themes with some argument and dispute thrown ın for good measure. He had time for such writing because his work, though improving, was still not going as well as he had hoped. He earned £154 in his first year, £250 in his second and £300 in the next. This was good money for a provincial doctor but not nearly as much as he was telling his mother he earned. He wrote to her each week and usually said that he was about to make something like £1000 a year. As a doctor he never came near to earning this sum. He had retained his housekeeper even though friends had advised him against the expense, he was eating more now and had regained his former weight and he was smoking far more than he ever did in the past. There wasn't much money left at the end of each week. But the work had its rewards. Sometimes it was darkly amusing.

'Then there was a very tall, horse-faced old lady with an extraordinary dignity of bearing. She would sit framed in the window of her little house, like the picture of a grande dame of the old regime. But every now and again she went on a wild burst, in the course of which she would skim plates out of the window at the passers-by. I was the only one who had influence over her at such times, for she was a haughty, autocratic old person. Once she showed an inclination to skim a plate at me also, but I quelled her by assuming a gloomy dignity as portentous as her own. She had some art treasures which she heaped upon me when she was what we will politely call "ill", but claimed back again the moment she was well. Once when she had been particularly troublesome I retained a fine lava jug, in spite of her protests, and I have got it yet.'[2]

But there were tragic, sombre episodes as well. 'I was called in by a poor woman to see her daughter. As I entered the humble sitting-room there was a small cot at one side, and by the gesture of the mother I understood that the sufferer was there. I picked up a candle and walking over I stooped over the little bed, expecting to see a child. What

I really saw was a pair of brown sullen eyes, full of loathing and pain, which looked up in resentment to mine. I could not tell how old the creature was. Long thin limbs were twisted and coiled in the tiny couch. The face was sane but malignant. "What is it?" I asked in dismay when we were out of hearing. "It's a girl," sobbed the mother. "She's nineteen. Oh! if God would only take her!" What a life for both! And how hard to face such facts and accept any of the commonplace explanations of existence!'[3]

Some of these dark, depressing moments were made more bearable by the arrival of Conan Doyle's young brother Innes, only ten years old at the time. Conan Doyle dressed the boy in a page's uniform, complete with shiny buttons and epaulettes, and his job was to open the door for the patients and act as a sort of servant, at least during working hours. After hours, together in the evening, the two brothers told each other stories of Edinburgh, ate their supper together at a small table, played and walked, chatted about their mother and siblings, and laughed a great deal. It was one of the relatively few times that Conan Doyle became close to another member of his family apart from his mother. He had spent so much time away at school, at university and then at sea that there was always a certain distance between him and his brother and sisters. Innes remained with his brother until 1885, when he went off to public school in Yorkshire. Conan Doyle missed him very much.

There were other developments in his personal life. He was something of a local celebrity, as doctor, sportsman and newspaper correspondent, and some of the mothers in Southsea were encouraging their daughters to meet this friendly-looking Scot who cut such a dashing figure on the cricket pitch. They did not know just how poor he was. Some of the daughters did know but they did not much care. A Miss Jeffers had been one suitor and another was Miss Welden, a stout young woman who, much to Conan Doyle's satisfaction, went off to Switzerland.

Another woman was more to his liking. He met Louise Hawkins through his work. In March 1885 a friend, Dr Pike, was nursing Jack Hawkins, a boy who had cerebral meningitis. The patient's mother was staying with him in a boarding-house and Pike was finding it increasingly difficult to look after the boy. Conan Doyle was asked if he would be interested in taking over the case by putting the boy up in his house. He had the room, he had the time and he had the inclination. He cared for the boy with all the skill and compassion he had but he knew from the very beginning that the case was impossible and that the best he could do was to ease the child's suffering. Within days the boy was dead.

Jack's mother and sister were distraught but grateful. It was almost inevitable that Conan Doyle would strike up a friendship with the latter, a pleasant-looking if not beautiful young woman. Louise was a quiet girl, loyal to her family and anxious to settle down to a domestic life with a reliable husband. She had a round face and large, pretty eyes that stared quite charmingly when she was in conversation. Her nickname was 'Touie', and she was a competent pianist, a good singer and a talented sketch artist. She read novels but not newspapers and thought that Conan Doyle was extremely clever. It was not so much a love affair as a friendship that was intensely enjoyable for both of them. They appeared to agree about everything, or at least Louise did not disagree with her young man. Mary Doyle did not like Louise very much and thought her a bad choice for her son. No matter. In August 1885 Conan Doyle and Louise Hawkins were married.

'In many ways my marriage marked a turning-point in my life. A bachelor, especially one who had been a wanderer like myself, drifts easily into Bohemian habits, and I was no exception,' he said. Louise brought financial help as well as domestic stability because she had an allowance of £100 a year from her family. But it was not the money but the solid base and the firmness and sense of the definite that now liberated Conan Doyle. It was an odd marriage and probably a rushed one, and Conan Doyle later regretted the decision, though he never betrayed a woman he genuinely liked. With marriage came less frenzied activity and more time for thought and reflection. He had been and still was interested in the world beyond, in something resembling theology, in a sort of premature spiritualism, since his trips to sea and he was now determined to know more. He was also deeply frustrated. 'I cannot look back upon those years with any spiritual satisfaction, for I was still in the valley of darkness. I had ceased to butt my head incessantly against what seemed to be an impenetrable wall . . . A dim light of dawn was to come to me soon in an uncertain way which was destined in time to spread and grow brighter.'

He had already heard an American medium back in 1880 and now decided that he needed to hear and know a little more. J. Horstead was a Portsmouth spiritualist leader and medium with a reputation in the area for being the conduit for the thoughts and words of John Wesley the founder of Methodism, and various dead Liberal politicians of the past fifty years. He had around forty loyal followers in the area and for some two years had operated quite successfully, occasionally speaking to groups of up to a hundred. These were moderate meetings lacking some of the dramatics and theatre of other mediums, at whose gatherings smoke and screaming would fill the hall. But Horstead was more trusted than some of his competitors and created a far healthier climate for his movement in that part of the country. With so many false mediums, fraudsters and amateurs around at the time, this man was a welcome relief.

With the formation of the Society for Psychical Research in 1882 there was a proliferation of small groups and a wave of interest in spiritualism. Conan Doyle was fortunate enough in having not only Horstead but the man's spiritualist successor in Portsmouth, Major-General Alfred W. Drayson. This former army officer was a man after his own heart, with a passion for whist, spiritualism, military history and writing. He had written books on astronomy and card-playing and been published in some of the same periodicals as Conan Doyle, including *Every Boy's Magazine*. This was a meeting of minds, a mingling of ectoplasms. Drayson also worked to develop in Conan Doyle an interest in mesmerism, a pseudo-science of which he had been aware for some time.

Mesmerism was named after the eighteenth-century Austrian doctor Friedrich Anton Mesmer. From his studies in Vienna and in southern Germany Mesmer had concluded that the planets had an effect on human beings and their actions through an electrical force and that this could be influenced or controlled by the power and pull of magnets. He earned a great deal of money and became a celebrity simply by running magnets along the bodies of the wealthy sick and convincing them that they were cured. He even had them wear clothes with small magnets sewn into the lining. In the year before the French Revolution he moved to Paris, where, his timing being less fortunate than his powers to convince, he became a favourite of Louis XVI and Marie Antoinette. After some initial success he lost the trust of Parisian society and moved back to Vienna. Again, bad timing. He was arrested as a spy and spent two months in prison. He eventually chose to live in exile in Switzerland, where he died in 1815.

Mesmer's name was worth even more when he was dead than when he had been alive. A society of followers continued to investigate various medical, scientific and astronomical phenomena along similar lines and one man in particular, the Marquis de Puysegur and his helper, Deleuse, laid the foundations for hypnosis as we know it today. The idea became popular in Britain around the middle of the nineteenth century, when at London's University College Hospital Dr John Elliotson published a magazine called *The Zoist*, devoted to hypnotism and related subjects. From London the movement travelled north to Manchester and then to Glasgow and Edinburgh. It was in the latter city that Dr James Braid, based both in Scotland and in Manchester, was known as a successful and convincing exponent of hypnosis in his work. Braid had also been influenced by one Baron von Reichenbach – the name was learnt early by Conan Doyle and, on the evidence of his Sherlock Holmes stories, was never forgotten – who had defined and improved upon the original ideas of hypnosis and so-called magnetic powers. Reichenbach believed that it was only particularly sensitive people who could be affected by magnetism and that decomposing bodies gave off a special luminescence, accounting for sightings of ghosts in graveyards. Not surprisingly, most doctors rejected many of his ideas, but many of them were intrigued by the possibilities of hypnosis, both to calm or anaesthetize patients and to discover pertinent facts about their background when they entered the deepest hypnotic state.

By the 1880s two doctors, Liebault and Bernheim, had popularized and refined hypnosis and Conan Doyle was following their work with growing interest. In 1884 the young doctor's story *John Barrington Cowles* was published in *Cassell's Saturday Journal*. The protagonist, Cowles, is a young medical student who studies in Scotland – there are many other clear resemblances to the author – and meets an evil female hypnotist who has already killed two of her lovers. The story might be badly organized but it does bring some sort of experience with hypnosis to bear, mingling it with ideas on sado-masochism.

The following year, just as he was about to marry Louise, Conan Doyle published *The Great Keinplatz Experiment*. This tale features a Professor von Baumgarten, who has all the best lines and seems to speak them directly for his creator. 'It is evident that under certain conditions the soul or mind does separate itself from the body. In the case of a mesmerised person, the body lies in a cataleptic condition, but the spirit has left it. Perhaps you reply that the soul is there, but in a dormant condition. I answer that this is not so, otherwise how can one account for the condition of clairvoyance, which has fallen into disrepute through the knavery of certain scoundrels, but which can easily be shown to be an undoubted fact. I have been able myself, with a sensitive subject, to obtain an accurate description of what was going on in another room or another house. How can such knowledge be accounted for on any hypothesis save that the soul of the subject has left the body and is wandering through space? For a moment it is recalled by the voice of the operator and says what it has seen and then wings its way once more through the air. Since the spirit is by its very nature invisible, we cannot see these comings and goings, but we see their effect in the body of the subject, now rigid and inert, now struggling to narrate impressions which could never have come to it by natural means.'

Through the social connections of his new wife Louise, Conan Doyle met a group of people who were convinced spiritualists and participated in one of their seances. He was ambivalent about what he had seen. The table moved, messages were delivered, the other people present seemed to be utterly convinced by what was going on. What took Conan Doyle in the direction of belief was not this but the influence and intelligence of Alfred Drayson. This experienced and hardened soldier and administrator was just the sort of man to convert him. He was a no-nonsense figure, phlegmatic and reliable, but also something of a romantic. Conan Doyle began to regard Drayson as a genius, 'a very distinguished thinker and a pioneer of psychic knowledge'.[4] Under the man's influence he began to read the spiritualist journal, *Light*, and attended further seances. Some of them were obviously stage-managed, sometimes ridiculously so, with ropes and pulleys clearly visible behind and above apparitions, and voices emanating from behind cupboard doors rather than from the heavens. Drayson reassured Conan Doyle that fraud was just as common in spiritualism as anywhere else – why should it not be? – but this had no bearing on its validity or truth. Were there not people who claimed to be Christians who in fact lived uncharitable and hateful lives? This neither proved Christianity to be a lie nor made it in any way more truthful. Personal error and hypocrisy were irrelevant.

Drayson also led Conan Doyle towards the periphery of Buddhism, and in particular towards the ideas of reincarnation and karma. Madame Blavatsky was a key figure here, one of a group of late-nineteenth-century exotics who claimed the ability to summon visitations from the world beyond and also to possess special powers. Her reputation was shattered when a leading member of the Theosophical Society, Richard Hodgson, showed some of her claims to be completely unfounded. There were so many rival views, so much new information, and at this stage Conan Doyle was reading everything he could get his hands on, while Louise was equally fascinated if not quite as diligent. He felt that to be completely convinced he would have to hold a seance in his own house with people he knew, and in comfortable and trusted surroundings with no hidden passages or disguised entrances. These seances were, again, merely promising and not the stuff of definite proof.

'I have no psychical powers myself, and those who worked with me had little more. Among us we could just muster enough of the magnetic force, or whatever you will call it, to get the table movements with their suspicious and often stupid messages. I still have notes of those sittings and copies of some, at least, of the messages. They were not always absolutely stupid. For example, I find that on one occasion, on my asking some test question, such as how many coins I had in my pocket, the table spelt out: "We are here to educate and to elevate, not to guess riddles." And then: "The religious frame of mind, not the critical, is what we wish to inculcate." Now, no one could say that that was a puerile message. On the other hand, I was always haunted by the fear of involuntary pressure from the hands of the sitters.'

Drayson also asked Conan Doyle to attend some of his

own seances and these proved to be much more satisfying. But there was still a credibility gap and Conan Doyle still refused to make the great leap. Drayson knew enough about bringing new people into the fold to realize that he had achieved a great deal with the young man but that it was now time for someone else to take over the course of instruction. He put him in contact with another member of the Literary and Scientific Society, a man named Henry Ball. Drayson and Ball had conducted psychic experiments together and studied texts on the subject. Now Ball took Conan Doyle under his wing and they attended seances, sometimes joined by Drayson.

Conan Doyle must have seen something that impressed him very much because by July 1887 he was able, and willing, to write to *Light* and declare his interest and belief. The letter is one of the most important he ever wrote and is worth quoting at some length. After recounting some of his feelings and readings he stated: 'I could no more doubt the existence of the phenomena than I could doubt the existence of lions in Africa, though I have been to that continent and have never chanced to see one. I felt that if human evidence – regarding both the quantity and the quality of the witnesses – can prove anything, it has proved this.' After referring to his own semi-successful experiments he continued to tell his tale. He is not always completely honest – for example, this was not the first time he had attended a seance with an experienced medium. 'Last week I was invited by two friends to join them in a sitting with an old gentleman who was reputed to have considerable mediumistic power. It was the first time I had ever had the opportunity of sitting with anyone who was not a novice and inquirer like myself. I may remark here that for some days I had been debating in my mind whether I should get a copy of Leigh Hunt's *Comic Dramatists of the Restoration* – the question being whether the mental pollution arising from Messrs. Congreve, Wycherley, and Co. would be compensated for by the picture of the manners and customs of those days to be gathered from their pages, and which I had particular reasons for wishing to be well up in. I had thought the matter over, but had dismissed it from my mind a day or two before the seance. On sitting, our medium came quickly under control, and delivered a trance address, containing much interesting and elevating matter. He then became clairvoyant, describing one or two scenes which we had no opportunity of testing. So far, the meeting had been very interesting, but not above the possibility of deception. We then proposed writing. The medium took up a pencil, and after a few convulsive movements, he wrote a message to each of us. Mine ran: "This gentleman is a healer. Tell him from me not to read Leigh Hunt's book." Now, sir, I can swear that no one knew I had contemplated reading that book, and, moreover, it was no case of thought-reading, for I had never referred to the matter all day. I can only say that if I had had to devise a test message I could not have hit upon one which was so absolutely inexplicable on any hypothesis except that held by Spiritualists. The message of one of my friends, referring to his own private affairs, was as startlingly correct as mine.

'Let me conclude by exhorting any other searcher never to despair of receiving personal testimony, but to persevere through any number of failures until at last conviction comes to him, as come it will. Let him deserve success by his patience and earnestness, and he will gain it. Above all, let every inquirer bear in mind that phenomena are only a means to an end, of no value at all of themselves, and simply useful as giving us assurance of an after existence for which we are to prepare by refining away our grosser animal feelings and cultivating our higher, nobler impulses. Unless a man starts with the idea the seance-room sinks to the level of the theatre or the opera – a mere idle resort for the indulgence of a foolish, purposeless curiosity. Let a man realise that the human soul, as it emerges from its bodily cocoon, shapes its destiny in exact accordance with its condition; that that condition depends upon the sum result of his actions and thoughts on this life; that every evil deed stamps itself upon the spirit and entails its own punishment with the same certainty that a man stepping out of a second floor window falls to the ground; that there is no room for deathbed repentances or other nebulous conditions which might screen the evil doer from the consequence of his own deeds, but that the law is self-acting and inexorable. This, I take it, is the lesson which Spiritualism enforces, and all phenomena are only witnesses to the truth of this central all-important fact.'[5]

The letter is significant and central in two ways. It marks Conan Doyle's coming of age as a spiritualist in his own terms, an acknowledgement that he believed in the movement. More important, it was also a public declaration that this was where he stood, this was his belief, and if anybody opposed him they knew what to expect and what to challenge. It was a courageous act because spiritualism was not taken seriously by everybody and though not openly mocked as it is today it was nevertheless thought to be on the edge of foolishness. There was a strong move within the medical profession to parody and marginalize it until it was virtually impossible for a doctor to continue to practise if he held such views. But Conan Doyle had placed his flag quite firmly in the ground and dared all who disagreed with him to come forward. He was now a spiritualist and the belief would, without doubt, become the most important cause of his life.

If Conan Doyle had finally been pulled by the twitch upon the spiritualist thread he was also immersing himself in reading that ranged from the history of railways to eighteenth-century novels, accounts of travels in China to guides to bird-watching. He read with a butterfly mind, settling on a particular flower of a subject, taking from it the nourishment he needed at the time and then immediately moving elsewhere without a backward glance. In the process he read a large number of detective novels and what constantly struck him was the meagre nature of so many of them. The characters were often weak and clichéd, the plots were generally formulaic and unimaginative and, worst of all, the solutions to the mysteries were completely unsatisfying. The detectives, in all their manifestations, caught their criminals and solved their crimes but gave the reader hardly any line of thought or logical reasoning behind their success. The stories were full of clumsy coincidences, last-minute confessions and ridiculous mistakes by the crimes' perpetrators.

If Conan Doyle was anything he was thorough and conscientious and he saw in the detective genre a gaping hole. 'Gaboriau had rather attracted me by the neat dovetailing of his plots, and Poe's masterful detective, M. Dupin, has from boyhood been one of my heroes. But could I bring an addition of my own?' He had heard true-life stories of the underworld and come into contact with some its denizens when he had worked as a surgeon at sea, and also when he had treated very poor patients in Birmingham, Plymouth and Portsmouth. Conan Doyle's decision to become a writer of detective stories was purely professional, based on an intelligent observation of the market and a clear understanding of his own literary capabilities and limitations. We should not, however, confuse the businesslike with the prosaic.

The same applied to his choice of a name for his new creation. If he was to write about a detective the man would have to have an exotic name, one that stuck in the mind and injected the character with a certain ambiguity and charisma. Again, Conan Doyle learnt this from his predecessors. He came up with Sherrinford Holmes, whose adventures would be told by Ormond Sacker. The two men would make their debut in a story called 'A Tangled Skein'. But no. The names were rejected as being too long and too obscure. Conan Doyle tried several variations of title and eventually settled on 'A Study in Scarlet'. He had trouble with Ormond Sacker and instead chose the simple and refreshing Dr John Watson. Conan Doyle's hero 'could not tell his own exploits, so he must have a commonplace comrade as a foil' wrote his creator. 'An educated man of action who could both join in the exploits and narrate them. A drab, quiet name for this unostentatious man. Watson would do.' As for Sherrinford Holmes, the surname was fine but there was something not quite right about the Sherrinford. Too long, too many syllables. Shorter, crisper. He had it: Sherlock. The detective would be Sherlock Holmes. Arthur Conan Doyle was not yet twenty-eight years old.

When the manuscript introducing these two men was finished Conan Doyle sent it off to the man who had published some of his earlier material, James Payn. Payn was an experienced journalist and editor. A graduate of Trinity College, Cambridge, he had begun as a freelance writer for publications such as *Household Words* and then became the editor first of *Chambers' Journal* and then, between 1882 and 1896, of the *Cornhill Magazine*. He was also a poet and essayist and wrote more than a hundred novels, the best of which were *By Proxy* and *Lost Sir Massinberd*. He knew his business. But not this time. He rejected the work, explaining that it was too short for serialization and too long to be printed as a single magazine piece. This might not have been the real reason because he added the strange apology: 'I have kept your story an unconscionably long time.'

Conan Doyle was never particularly sensitive or vulnerable to literary criticism unless he had complete confidence in the source from which it came. He was hurt but not influenced by failure. In May 1886 he sent his detective story to Arrowsmith, who returned it two months later without having read it, then to Warne, then to two other publishers. Finally he sent the book to Ward, Lock & Co, who had a reputation for publishing popular if not always high-quality material. They agreed to pay him £25 and when he asked for more they told him that there were to be no negotiations. So small was the amount of money that he seriously considered turning it down. But he was poor and extremely anxious for the work, for any work, to be published. He would never see another penny for the book. 'We have read your story and are pleased with it,' they wrote in October. 'We could not publish it this year as the market is flooded at present with cheap fiction.'

His approach to his first Sherlock Holmes story was the same one as Conan Doyle adopted throughout his career as a writer of detective tales. He wrote them and then let them go. His involvement in the process after the first version had been submitted to his publisher was surprisingly meagre. We can only speculate on how much editing and change took place in the period between Conan Doyle writing his last words and the story appearing in print. He didn't complain. He wanted it that way. In a letter to his fellow detective writer G.K. Chesterton he explained that although the Holmes stories could be improved by editing, the basic plot and dialogue could not be made better by him; he had given his all in his first effort and everything after that would be gratuitous and a waste of time.[6]

A 'Study in Scarlet' eventually appeared in *Beeton's Christmas Annual* of 1887. There were not many reviews but the entire print run sold out. Even then the publishers were mean with their praise, although they did know potential profit when they saw it. The work was reprinted as a single volume by Ward, Lock & Co in July 1888, with illustrations drawn by the author's father, Charles Doyle. But it was not the illustrations that people were interested in. 'In the year 1878 I took my degree of Doctor of Medicine of the University of London, and proceeded to Netley to go through the course prescribed for surgeons in the army,' wrote Conan Doyle. And later in the book: '"Dr Watson, Mr Sherlock Holmes," said Stanford, introducing us.

"How are you?" he said cordially, gripping my hand with a strength for which I should hardly have given him credit. "You have been in Afghanistan, I perceive."'

The *Glasgow Herald* wrote about the work in December 1887: '*Beeton's Christmas Annual* (London: Ward, Lock & Co.) is now an old institution, and as regularly looked for as the holly and mistletoe. This year its contents are full and varied. The piece de resistance is a story by A. Conan Doyle entitled "A Study in Scarlet". It is the story of a murder, and of the preternatural sagacity of a scientific detective, to whom Edgar Allan Poe's Dupin was a trifler, and Gaboriau's Lecoq a child. He is a wonderful man is Mr Sherlock Holmes, but one gets so wonderfully interested in his cleverness and in the mysterious murder which he unravels that one cannot lay down the narrative until the end is reached. What that end is wild horses shall not make us divulge. After the "Study in Scarlet" come two original little drawing-room plays. One is of the nature of a vaudeville, and is called "Food for Powder"; it should be effective as it is amusing. The other is "The Four-Leaved Shamrock", a drawing-room comedietta in three acts, also very good of its kind. The number is enriched with engravings by D.H. Friston, Matt Streetch, and R. Andre.'

Holmes was heavily influenced by Dr Joseph Bell, and was in part Conan Doyle, but he was mostly the sum of the author's imagination and literary skill. Those critics who are convinced that Holmes was simply a caricature of Bell or just the *alter ego* of his creator have done enormous damage to Conan Doyle's reputation as a writer. Every character is a composite of the influences on the author and a reflection of his identity. But each is still a creation. Conan Doyle gave birth to Sherlock Holmes, fed him and saw that he grew to maturity. He brought to bear the usual skills involved in fiction and characterization. As for those people who believe that somehow Holmes was a real person and Conan Doyle a mere conduit, they are to be pitied.

The title of the first book refers to Holmes's comment about 'the scarlet thread of murder running through the colourless skein of life'. 'A Study in Scarlet' is in two parts, the first being Dr Watson's memories of his time in the army, his meeting with Sherlock Holmes and the murder of Enoch Drebber and Joseph Strangerson by Jefferson Hope. The second part is called 'The Country of the Saints' and is about the Mormons of Utah between 1847 and 1860. The book ends with Watson again, telling of Jefferson Hope's confession and Holmes's explanation of how he solved the murders. Conan Doyle obviously knew very little about the Mormons because the information about their religion and past is profoundly wrong. Yet that does not seem to matter very much.

But even at this early stage, and certainly later in Conan Doyle's career, he was more concerned with other matters than Sherlock Holmes. Spiritualism was inevitably a driving force, and in his literary career he was intent on establishing himself as a historical novelist. He started researching and planning the background to *Micah Clarke* in the summer of 1887 and the novel was published two years later. The story is set in the late seventeenth century, when the Catholic King James II was attempting to reintroduce Roman Catholicism into England. The Duke of Monmouth rose up against James and was eventually defeated in 1685 at the Battle of Sedgemoor, which is depicted in the book. The action scenes are drawn well, including a fight inside the thirteenth-century Wells Cathedral. Nor are the characters neglected. Micah Clarke himself and his father, Joe Clarke, an old fighting man who served under Cromwell, are fleshed-out, convincing figures, if a little archaic. But that was the flavour of the book. Even its full title was painted with the brush of mock authenticity and pseudo-antiquity: 'Micah Clarke His Statement as Made to His Three Grand-Children Joseph, Hervas & Reuben During the Hard Winter of 1734 Wherein is Contained a Full Report of Certain Passages in His Early Life Together with Some Account of His Journey from Havant to Taunton with Decimus Saxon in the Summer of 1685. Also of the Adventures that Befell Them During the Western Rebellion, & of their Intercourse with James Duke of Monmouth, Lord Grey, & Other Persons of Quality Compiled Day by Day, from His Own Narration, by Joseph Clarke, & Never Previously Set Forth in Print. Now for the First Time Collected, Corrected, & Re-Arranged from the Original Manuscripts by A. Conan Doyle.'

Conan Doyle was an admirer of Oliver Cromwell and the Puritans, who by force of arms and will defeated their royalist opponents and imposed a new kind of government on England. They exhibited the qualities of strength, courage, integrity and fervour that he appreciated in his historical figures. This affection for the parliamentarians of the Civil War was also in part a reaction by Conan Doyle to his Roman Catholic education, for he had been told by his Jesuit teachers that the Cromwellians were immoral extremists who murdered innocent Catholics and, perish the thought, took away the people's Christmas puddings. Though Conan Doyle always liked Christmas puddings he had responded by reading as much as he could about the military victories of the New Model Army and of the history of the Commonwealth and Protectorate.

Lord Macaulay influenced his sense of history and Sir Walter Scott his sense of fiction. But mostly he was influenced by his own sense of what was right and what had happened many years ago, something that had been with him since he was a small boy. Whenever he visited a new place, or walked along a different road, he would explore its historical significance and, just as important, imagine what might have happened there. He was determined never to be a prisoner of his own age, an age he did not particularly care for at that. This attitude was as much a factor in his spiritualist belief as it was in his writing. He enjoyed *Micah Clarke* not only because it was his first published historical novel but because he sincerely believed in the cause he had written about. He always thought the Stuart kings to be ungrateful men, meagre characters compared with the tough, able types who fought against them. He cited a passage by his beloved Macaulay, 'I cannot quote it verbally – in which he says that after the Restoration if ever you saw a carter more intelligent than his fellows, or a peasant who tilled his land better, you would be likely to find that it was an old pikeman of Cromwell's.'

The reaction to the book was at first very discouraging. James Payn, even though he had published some of Conan Doyle's earlier work, was a man who really should not go down in history as an expert judge of what constitutes popular and commercially profitable literature. He saw the manuscript and returned it to the author with an incredulous, almost angry, 'How can you, can you, waste your time and your wits writing historical novels!' Other publishers rejected it as well. Blackwood detected 'imperfections' and considered the work to have little chance of achieving any commercial success. What particularly annoyed Conan Doyle was that he regarded certain passages and aspects of the book as the best work he had ever done, and he thought the same until the end of his life. It is revealing that in his memoirs he says that the book sold well after Longman published it and also received some extremely good reviews. In fact it sold quite badly at first but picked up after the success of the later Sherlock Holmes stories, and while some of the reviews were remarkably good, others were mixed or worse.

It was in the United States that Conan Doyle's literary career would be given its impetus. In 1889 he was asked by the London agent of a magazine and book publisher in Pennsylvania, Lippincott, to provide them with another Sherlock Holmes story. A 'Study in Scarlet' had done extremely well in the United States but not to Conan Doyle's financial advantage. There was no copyright law for British work and immediately a book was published in London it was sent to New York, Chicago or Boston to be copied and republished, often on cheap paper, with ridiculous and inappropriate covers and even with errors and omissions. As Conan Doyle said of this, it was hard

on British writers but also on their American counter-
parts because of the unbridled competition such a system
gave them.

But Conan Doyle did not yet regard himself as a professional writer and was convinced that neither did other
people. Certainly he was not part of any genuine literary set,
partly because he did not live in London, partly because he
had not yet written very much and, most unfairly, because
of the genre of his work. The problem that would be
with him throughout his life – and live on beyond it –
had already begun. Conan Doyle the writer of detective
stories and historical romances was not taken sufficiently
seriously. It was indicative of his character and attitude that
this perception always bothered Conan Doyle's friends and
supporters more than it disturbed him. In fact he made light
of it. One of the few occasions he dined with a literary set
in his early career was when a dinner was arranged at the
Ship inn in Greenwich around the *Cornhill Magazine*, for
which Conan Doyle had been writing. 'All the authors and
artists were there, and I remember the reverence with which
I approached James Payn, who was to me the warden of the
sacred gate. I was among the first arrivals, and was greeted
by Mr Smith, the head of the firm, who introduced me to
Payn. I loved much of his work and waited in awe for the
first weighty remark which should fall from his lips. It was
that there was a crack in the window and he wondered how
the devil it had got there.'

Oddly enough, Oscar Wilde was one of the first writers in
that 'literary community' to see in Conan Doyle an immense
talent. Odd because Conan Doyle's intensely physical historical stories and aesthetically lightweight detective tales
were not the type of material Wilde usually championed.
The two met at a party thrown at the Langham Hotel by
Joseph Marshall Stoddart, managing editor of Lippincott's,
and for Conan Doyle it was 'a golden evening'. Wilde had
apparently read and enjoyed *Micah Clarke* and tried his best
to include Conan Doyle in the spirit of the gathering. 'His

conversation left an indelible impression upon my mind. He towered above us all, and yet had the art of seeming to be interested in all that we could say. He had delicacy of feeling and tact, for the monologue man, however clever, can never be a gentleman at heart. He took as well as gave, but what he gave was unique. He had a curious precision of statement, a delicate flavour of humour, and a trick of small gestures to illustrate his meaning, which were peculiar to himself. The effect cannot be reproduced, but I remember how in discussing the wars of the future he said: "A chemist on each side will approach the frontier with a bottle" – his upraised hand and precise face conjuring up a vivid and grotesque picture. His anecdotes, too, were happy and curious. We were discussing the cynical maxim that the good fortune of our friends made us discontented. "The devil," said Wilde, "was once crossing the Libyan desert, and he came upon a spot where a number of small fiends were tormenting a holy hermit. The sainted man easily shook off their evil suggestions. The devil watched their failure, and then he stepped forward to give them a lesson. 'What you do is too crude,' said he. 'Permit me for one moment.' With that he whispered to the holy man, 'Your brother has just been made Bishop of Alexandria.' A scowl of malignant jealousy at once clouded the serene face of the hermit. 'That,' said the devil to his imps, 'is the sort of thing which I should recommend.'" Conan Doyle had clearly met the genuine Oscar Wilde.

The evening was particularly portentous because by its conclusion both Wilde and Conan Doyle had agreed to write a book for *Lippincott's Magazine*. The former would produce *The Picture of Dorian Grey*, the latter *The Sign of Four*. The contract for Conan Doyle's novel, dated 30 August 1889, was written on the same day that the meal took place, demonstrating just how anxious were the Americans to have another Sherlock Holmes story. Conan Doyle agreed to deliver a 40,000-word manuscript for the price of £100. The week after the dinner and the contract Conan Doyle wrote to Stoddart explaining that his new story would be titled either *The Sign of Six* or *The Problem of the Sholtos*. In the end it was given neither title.

The Sign of Four appeared in *Lippincott's Magazine* for February 1890 and was published in book form shortly afterwards. The story takes place in London – still a city relatively unknown to Conan Doyle – and concerns a mystery, recounted by a Miss Mortan, that has taken place in a large, strange house in the suburbs, by the name of Pondicherry Lodge. The woman has been receiving gifts of pearls without any explanation and has now received a bewildering message. After Holmes begins his investigation a murder takes place, that of Major Bartholomew Sholto (almost certainly a character modelled on Oscar Wilde). Holmes solves all only after two exciting chases – one with his trusted dog Toby, used only on special occasions for the purpose of sniffing a scent – and another along the Thames, after Jonathan Small and hidden treasure.

Small, who is well drawn, is one of Conan Doyle's ambivalent criminals. He was originally a soldier and plantation overseer in India – the heat and horror of the era are conveyed very well, influenced by Conan Doyle's travels to Africa rather than any experience of India itself – who turned to crime during the Indian Mutiny of 1854 when he joined three Sikhs in the theft of the Agra treasure. He was caught and sent to the Andaman Islands to serve out his punishment, but escaped and searched for the treasure that was now in the hands of Major Sholto. Small is aided by an improbable but still unforgettable Andaman Islander who actually murders Sholto. Holmes fires his gun at the little man on the Thames – being the only time the detective shoots at a person in any of the Conan Doyle stories.

The story provides the opportunity for Dr Watson to become romantically involved with Mary Mortan, for the relationship between Holmes and Watson to be given more substance and for the domestic lives of the two men to develop. For the first time the reader sees Holmes in his Baker Street castle, protected and cushioned from the outside world but always ready to ride out to do battle with the forces of evil. This comfortable bachelor life with two good friends dining alone and relying on the services of good old, fussing old, characterless old Mrs Hudson shielded Holmes not only from external pressures but from sexual and personal concerns. It was all extremely artificial but it was also the ideal setting for the master detective, reluctant as Conan Doyle was to muddy his criminal waters with too much intimate detail or involvement with other characters who might detract from the plot or from the towering personalities of Holmes and Watson. By the end of the book Watson tells Holmes that he intends to get married but this is little more than a temporary interruption in their relationship.

There are, unfortunately, some errors and mistakes in the book, as there were in almost all Conan Doyle's works. The plot moves from June to September within hours and without any explanation or reason. And without any subsequent apology, because Conan Doyle was reluctant to dwell on such matters after a book had been published. The descriptions of Tonga and, less forgivably, London are often very inaccurate, the latter due to the fact that Conan Doyle often used a map book rather than first-hand knowledge for his earlier writings about the imperial capital he claimed to know so well. There is also a problem of names. The three Sikh characters in the book, Mahomet Singh, Abdullah Khan and Dost Akbar, all have Islamic names, an oversight which caused the author some embarrassment.

But these are small and, in the wider context of the book and its characters, minor difficulties. *The Sign of Four* established the great detective and many of his eccentricities and foibles. It also established Conan Doyle. It deserved to. The book begins with: 'Sherlock Holmes took his bottle from the corner of the mantelpiece, and his hypodermic syringe from its neat morocco case. With his long, white, nervous fingers he adjusted the delicate needle, and rolled back his left shirt-cuff. For some little time his eyes rested thoughtfully upon his sinewy forearm and wrist, all dotted and scarred with innumerable puncture-marks. Finally, he thrust the sharp point home, pressed down the tiny piston, and sank back into the velvet-lined arm-chair with a long sigh of satisfaction.

'Three times a day for many months I had witnessed this performance, but custom had not reconciled my mind to it. On the contrary, from day to day I had become more irritable at the sight and my conscience swelled nightly within me at the thought that I had lacked the courage to protest. Again and again I had registered a vow that I should deliver my soul upon the subject; but there was that in the cool, nonchalant air of my companion which made him the last man with whom one would care to take anything approaching to a liberty. His great powers, his masterly manner, and the experience which I had of his many extraordinary qualities, all made me diffident and backward in crossing him.'

The passage has repeatedly led to the question of whether Conan Doyle himself ever formed an addiction to a stimulant or a narcotic. Speculation abounds but evidence does not. He was familiar with most types of drugs from his medical training, had witnessed addiction from his days on board a ship and from his time as a doctor dealing with drug-addicted patients. He had been injected with hallucinogenic drugs during illnesses but was never an addict of any kind. It is one of the great tragedies of Conan Doyle's life, and afterlife, that his own personality has been partly lost because of the exponential growth of the fictional character that he created.

The reviews of *The Sign of Four* generally agreed on the success of the story and were very good, but there were some notices that gave their rash authors just enough rope. An unsigned critic in the *Athenaeum* wrote on 6 December 1890: 'A detective story is usually lively reading, but we cannot pretend to think that *The Sign of Four* is up to the level of the writer's best work. It is a curious medley, and full of horrors; and surely those who play hide and seek with the fatal treasure are a curious company. The wooden-legged convict and his fiendish misshapen little mate, the ghastly twins, the genial prizefighters, the detectives wise and foolish, and the gentle girl whose lover tells the tale, twist in and out together in a mazy dance, culminating in that mad and terrible rush down the river which ends in mystery and the treasure. Dr Doyle's admirers will read the little volume through eagerly enough, but they will hardly care to take it up again.' Praise be to anonymity.

And praise be to Conan Doyle's apparently inexhaustible energy at this stage of his life. He was determined to exploit his success and gave himself a daunting regimen. He went to bed late, always intrigued by the small hours, but was usually at work by 7.30 in the morning. He experimented with sleep deprivation, sometimes surviving on four hours a night, but found that this was only possible when work was going particularly well. Failure or writer's block made him more tired. He also smoked more and ate less when he was working hard. As a mature man he gained weight and was always conscious of his tendency to look plump in photographs. On one occasion he bought two identical suits, a smaller one for when he was fit and a larger one for when he had added some weight.[7] But whatever his health or frame of mind he always worked at a tremendous rate and planned and began almost as many books as he completed.

One of the results of this great strength and stamina was another historical novel, *The White Company*, published in 1890. 'It seemed to me that the days of Edward III constituted the greatest epoch in English history – an epoch when both the French and the Scottish kings were prisoners in London,' he wrote.[8] 'This result had been brought about mainly by the powers of a body of men who had never been drawn in British literature, for though Scott treated in his inimitable way the English archer, it was as an outlaw rather than as a soldier that he drew him. I had some views of my own, too about the Middle Ages which I was anxious to set forth. I was familiar with Froissart and Chaucer and I was aware that the famous knights of old were by no means the athletic heroes of Scott, but were often of a very different type.' Hence came *The White Company* and, published sixteen years later but the earlier book in terms of historical chronology, *Sir Nigel*. The former was, explained Conan Doyle to *The Bookman* in 1893, the product of extensive research and the reading of over a hundred books, particularly W. Longman's *Life and Times of Edward III*, published more than twenty years earlier.

The White Company is a detailed study of English and French life and ways in the fourteenth century and it is this background that provides the best aspects of the novel. However, the plot is poor and the lack of sufficiently strong characters – it was Conan Doyle's tragedy that he never equalled Holmes and Watson – meant that the story could not be saved. The young Alleyne Edricson leaves the abbey of Beaulieu in the New Forest to fight in France for Sir Nigel Loring and eventually returns to England to find true love. One of the most picturesque episodes in the book is a heroic battle that takes place in Spain, where the eponymous White Company is destroyed while fighting a valiant but futile action. The weapons and tactics used in the battle are authentic but Conan Doyle apparently could not resist throwing in a caricature or a historical cliché, ruining all his efforts to create medieval verisimilitude. The most satisfying character in the book is Sir Nigel Loring, who returns in the novel bearing his name.

Conan Doyle was more nervous about the reception of *The White Company* than that of almost any other of his books. 'I remember that as I wrote the last words . . . I felt a wave of exultation and with a cry of "That's done it!" I hurled my inky pen across the room, where it left a black smudge upon the duck's-egg wall-paper.' It was almost inevitable. As the reviews appeared the author's concerns and apprehensions were proved correct. *The White Company* sold well and continued to do so for another forty years – though it is now severely out of fashion – but many critics found it difficult to take the book seriously. Conan Doyle wrote to friends and to his mother, complaining that reviewers did not understand his purpose in writing it. He was trying to illuminate the nation's traditions, he insisted, and critics mocked him. Sales and profits from the book never managed to compensate Conan Doyle for its poor reception.

The dent in his confidence and character was never fully repaired. Thirty years later Conan Doyle wrote of *The White Company* and *Sir Nigel*: 'I have no hesitation in saying that the two of them taken together did thoroughly achieve my purpose, that they made an accurate picture of that great age.' And then, explaining the sense of failure that infected his later years: 'They form the most complete, satisfying and ambitious thing that I have ever done. All things find their level, but I believe that if I had never touched Holmes, who has tended to obscure my higher work, my position in literature would at the present moment be a more commanding one.'

The entire episode of *The White Company*, Conan Doyle's understanding of it and his chagrin and shock at the subsequent reviews, shows just how naive and unworldly the author could be. Even the conclusion of the book is mawkish and stiff: 'The sky may darken, and the clouds may gather, and again the day may come when Britain may have sore need of her children, on whatever shore of the sea they be found. Shall they not muster at her call.' Throughout the text there are intrusions of arcane language and anachronistic gestures and comments, clearly extensions of Conan Doyle's concepts of honour and examples of his own beliefs rather than convincing portrayals of medieval behaviour or even actions consistent with the novel's heroes.

An interesting side-note is that the British Union of Fascists recommended *The White Company* to its members in the early 1930s and even quoted the book's final paragraph in its propaganda. Clearly it appealed to their raw, clumsy understanding of patriotism. We know that Conan Doyle never knew of this. We should be glad that he didn't.

He was now thirty-one, a well-known author with a growing reputation and a quiet, happy married life. The times had been kind to him. Failures and losses seemed to be balanced by successes and joy. In 1890 his sister Annette died but only months earlier Conan Doyle and Louise had had a daughter, Mary Louise. She was baptized in an Anglican church and Conan Doyle's mother came down from Yorkshire to attend the ceremony. Mother, wife, child, career – stability. Yet contrary to what some think of Conan Doyle, this was no model of late-Victorian contentment, if such a thing ever genuinely existed. The man had a deeply felt need for travel, adventure and fresh challenge. He would find them where he could. When he was lucky they did not get him into very much trouble.

3

Bohemia and Beyond

There had been many reports in the press in 1890 about Dr Robert Koch, a highly respected Berlin bacteriologist, having found a cure for tuberculosis with something called lymphinoculation. Conan Doyle had treated patients, in Britain and abroad, for most diseases and ailments but had no special interest in TB in spite of its devastating effects on so many people in late-nineteenth-century Europe. Yet he wrote that 'a great urge came upon me suddenly that I should go to Berlin' and preambled this statement with a protest that as the 'simple things of life have always been the most pleasant to me, it is possible that I should have remained in Southsea permanently . . .' The word 'protest' is used advisedly, in that he seemed to be doing it just a little too much.

There was in fact no reason for Conan Doyle to leave England and his family at this time, no reason for him to go to Germany to observe a medical treatment in which he had very little interest; unless, of course, he was bored with domestic life, uneasy with his wife and unsure of how he felt about his baby daughter. He was a kind father and a considerate husband for most of his life but this decision was thoughtless and selfish, an act of escapism if not one motivated by something even more irresponsible. He left a young wife with a young child and 'at a few hours' notice

I packed up a bag and started off alone upon this curious adventure'.

Conan Doyle managed to convince the *Review of Reviews* to commission him to write a pen-portrait of Koch, a man who was not renowned for his modesty. He eventually managed to see the bacteriologist, in spite of the enormous number of journalists and doctors around him and the wretched patients coming from all over Europe like pathetic pilgrims travelling as a last hope to any shrine that would offer even a glimpse of health or salvation. Some of these people actually died *en route* to Berlin, being found dead in their carriages when their trains finally arrived in the German capital. Conan Doyle was disappointed, even outraged, by some of what he saw, and argued vehemently with Koch's acolytes that they promised too much and provided too little to desperate people. It all seemed to be a grotesque circus rather than a scientific gathering. He later described what happened on the trip, and the result is almost reminiscent of Jerome K. Jerome at his most sardonic.

'Next day I went down to the great building where the address was to be given and managed by bribing the porter to get into the outer Hall. The huge audience was assembling in a room beyond. I tried further bribing that I might be slipped in, but the official became abusive. People streamed past me, but I was always the waiter at the gate. Finally every one had gone in and then a group of men came bustling across, Bergmann, bearded and formidable, in the van, with a tail of house surgeons and satellites behind him. I threw myself across his path. "I have come a thousand miles," said I. "May I not come in?" He halted and glared at me through his spectacles. "Perhaps you would like to take my place," he roared, working himself up into that strange folly of excitement which seems so strange in the heavy German nature. "This is the only place left. Yes, yes, take my place by all means. My classes are filled with Englishmen already." He fairly spat the word "Englishmen".'[1]

Conan Doyle learnt that the Koch team had argued with various British doctors over their medical experiments and their treatment of patients and that the natural allies in Europe were once again at each other's throats. But he did manage to see an American doctor's notes of the lecture and eventually, on 17 November 1890, from Berlin's Central Hotel, wrote a brave and accurate account of the whole extravaganza to the *Daily Telegraph*. The letter appeared in the newspaper three days later. 'It may, perhaps, be not entirely out of place for an English physician who has had good opportunities of seeing the recent development of the treatment for tuberculosis in Berlin to say something as to its present treatment and probable results. Great as is Koch's discovery, there can be no question that our knowledge of it is still very incomplete, and that it leaves large issues open to question. The sooner that this is recognised the less chance will there be of serious disappointment among those who are looking to Berlin for a panacea for their own or their friends' ill-health.'

It was while on the train to Berlin that Conan Doyle had met a Harley Street doctor named Malcolm Morris who explained that he was doing rather well from his practice as a skin specialist. Morris advised Conan Doyle to leave Portsmouth as soon as he could and take an office in London. He advised that there was a need for eye specialists in the upper reaches of London medicine and that Conan Doyle should study in Vienna. There would be plenty of time for writing and for playing, said Morris, and more lucrative work as a doctor. As soon as he returned to Britain Conan Doyle went, as usual, to consult his mother. She agreed with the idea and said she would take her little granddaughter for a while because this time Conan Doyle really should take his wife with him to Europe. He said goodbye to his friends in Portsmouth, to the spiritualists, the writers, the amateur actors and the hopeful cricketers and footballers and set off for Austria. The couple arrived in Vienna on 5 January 1891.

It was one of those rash, ill-considered acts that occurred throughout Conan Doyle's life. He had not planned properly, not considered the requirements of studying in a German-speaking country and never considered how his wife might feel about it all. He spoke German from his schooldays but his medical vocabulary in that language was virtually non-existent. 'We found a modest pension which was within our means, and we put in a very pleasant four months, during which I attended eye lectures at the Krankenhaus, but could certainly have learned far more in London . . . No doubt "has studied in Vienna" sounds well in a specialist's record, but it is usually taken for granted that he has exhausted his own country before going abroad, which was by no means the case with me. Therefore, so far as eye work goes, my winter was wasted, nor can I trace any particular spiritual or intellectual advance. On the other hand I saw a little of gay Viennese society.'

To pay for the trip to Vienna and the time spent there Conan Doyle wrote a play about alchemy entitled *The Doings of Raffles Haw*. The remarkable thing about this less-than-accomplished work is not how poor it was but that he was able to sell it so relatively easily. He had reached a position where his work was bought just because of his name. As he became increasingly cynical about medicine and doctoring, his reputation as an author steadily rose.

With the first half of the advice given him on the train to Berlin attempted, if not completed, Conan Doyle decided to complete the proposal and set up as a specialist in London. He took rooms at 23 Montague Place, behind the British Museum, and for £120 rented a large medical area and part of a waiting-room at 2 Upper Wimpole Street between Devonshire Street and Wimpole Street. Friends asked him why he was still bothering to work as a doctor, for he had not done very well at it so far and clearly did not have any particular appetite for it. He replied that he could not leave any work half finished. He had come this far, he would go a little further. But his protests became ever weaker.

The practice was soon going as badly as his others and there were times when the basic rent and expenses were not being covered by fees from London's wealthier sick people. Conan Doyle was also bored, experiencing a sense of ennui as soon as he finished his brisk walk from home to work. Medicine was a waste of time even more than it was a waste of money, particularly as his books – the two Sherlock Holmes stories and *The White Company* – were doing well and showing no signs of fading into obscurity. Once again his mother advised him and this time so did his wife. Doctoring was making him unhappy and it was time to be realistic about his prospects.

In fact he had already made his decision. The day he moved into his consulting rooms he had started work on 'A Scandal in Bohemia', initially entitled 'A Scandal of Bohemia'. He had time on his hands, he had stories to tell and he wrote extremely quickly. Conan Doyle sent 'A Scandal in Bohemia' to his literary agent, Alexander Pollock Watt, on 3 April, 'A Case of Identity' was completed seven days later, on 20 April 'The Red-Headed League' was finished, and 'The Boscombe Valley Mystery' a week after that. If he had not been forced to bed with flu in the first week of May the stories would no doubt have continued at this startling pace. But the attack was bad enough to be life-threatening and for some days his wife feared for his survival. On recovering, however, he was back at his writing, even working sitting up in bed between bouts of sleep. On 18 May he completed 'The Five Orange Pips' and the sixth of these Sherlock Holmes short stories, 'The Man with the Twisted Lip', was completed in August. The reason for the hiatus between the two last stories was that the Conan Doyles had been busy moving from Montague Place to a villa at 12 Tennison Road, South Norwood, at an annual rent of £85. The move took some time as Conan Doyle was anxious to find a home where he could work in peace, enjoy a certain space but also be in the middle of town relatively quickly. He looked at several locations and houses but eventually decided on the south London suburb. 'There we settled down, and there I made my first effort to live entirely by my pen. It soon became evident that I had been playing the game well within my powers and that I should have no difficulty in providing a sufficient income. It seemed as if I had settled into a life which might be continuous.'[2]

The six short stories featuring Sherlock Holmes were for publication in the *Strand Magazine* and introduced a new literary genre, consisting of separate, self-contained stories featuring the same central and support characters. Conan Doyle received £25 for the first stories, £35 for the later ones. Herbert Greenhough Smith was one of the founders of the *Strand Magazine* and it was he who commissioned and edited Conan Doyle. His accounts of the relationship between Conan Doyle and the magazine vary, but they all include immediate enthusiasm at the reading of a new genius. 'Well I remember how, many years ago when the *Strand Magazine* was making its start in a tiny room at the top of a building in a street off the Strand – a sanctum approached through a room crammed with typewriters, with machines incessantly clicking – there came to me an envelope containing the first two stories of a series which were destined to become famous all over the world as *The Adventures of Sherlock Holmes*. What a God-send to an editor jaded with wading through reams of impossible stuff! The ingenuity of plot, the limpid clearness of style, the perfect art of telling a story!'[3]

An extraordinarily insightful judgement, written as it was, almost thirty years after the event. The truth is probably that the first story, 'A Scandal in Bohemia', was accepted and enjoyed but not particularly noticed. It appeared in the *Strand Magazine* in July 1891, under the overall title 'Adventures of Sherlock Holmes' and the heading 'Adventure 1 – A Scandal in Bohemia'. All six stories appeared in this manner and developed an increasingly eager and hungry readership. So much so that after the first half dozen were published the magazine was prepared to pay a great deal more for further instalments. At first Conan Doyle turned down the request, partly because he desperately needed a rest, but also because by now he was aware of just how successful and popular was his detective. He knew that the *Strand had* to have more stories and would pay more for any new ones. He reconsidered his decision and announced that if he could decide the length of the stories and if the magazine would pay him £50 for each story he might be willing to write some more. He could have asked for more money. In fact he could have asked for many things. The *Strand* accepted his terms immediately and by late October he had written two more stories for it: 'The Adventure of the Blue Carbuncle' and 'The Adventure of the Speckled Band'.

'A Scandal in Bohemia' is as notable for its revelations about one particular aspect of Sherlock Holmes's character as for any feat of detection. This is the story where Holmes admits to an admiration for a woman. 'To Sherlock Holmes she is always *the* woman. I have seldom heard him mention her under any other name,' it begins. 'In his eyes she eclipses and predominates the whole of her sex.' There is an operatic tone to the story and indeed Irene Adler, *the* woman, is an operatic contralto who has conducted an unfortunate affair with a monarch of unlikely and operatic stature. Blackmail is the crime in this tale and Holmes, in some ways, meets his equal. Too many efforts have been made, and too much time wasted, on attempting to ascertain who the figures involved in the fictional blackmail may have been and to establish the sexual underpinning Holmes's feelings for Irene Adler. As to the former, influences on this character could have been the Canadian singer Marie Louise Lajeunesse or even the great Australian Soprano Dame Nellie Melba, and the King of Bohemia could have been based on Ludwig I of Bavaria, who gave up his throne for the woman he loved. As to the latter, the sexuality of those involved in the search for answers here is probably more interesting than the sexual context or attitudes of Conan Doyle and his fictional detective.

One aspect of Irene Adler that does deserve attention is her Jewish-sounding surname. If the choice is deliberate, and it often was with Conan Doyle, it may represent the author's growing interest in Jews and Judaism, as evidenced by his meetings with Jewish intellectuals and spiritualists in Vienna and Jewish writers and thinkers in London. G.K. Chesterton wrote to him at the time about Jewish issues – this was before Chesterton went through his unsavoury period of affected anti-Semitism – and implied in his letter that Conan Doyle had referred to the name Adler being of Jewish descent in a previous note.[4]

Conan Doyle had a particular friendship with the Anglo-Jewish novelist and activist Israel Zangwill and in a letter dated 6 November 1905, on the subject of Jewish suffering and Zionism, in response to a letter from Zangwill after a major series of pogroms in Poland and the western Ukraine, he wrote: 'Pray excuse my delay – I have been exceedingly busy. I have thought much of your scheme for the resettlement of the refugee Jews – of course I entirely sympathise with it. It seems monstrous and inhuman that on all the face of God's earth there should be no resting place for these unhappy people, who driven out of one land are refused admission into all others. Their position is like the poor non-combatants in the middle ages, who were driven out of the besieged city by the garrison but refused a passage through their lines by the besiegers. I would do anything I could to help them to a permanent home. But the more one thinks of it the more the practical difficulties grow – no doubt the British Empire has many tropical or semi-tropical sites vacant for such a colony. There is East Africa – the Highlands of Uganda, Northern Rhodesia, New Guinea and doubtless many other places which I have not thought of.'[5] He went on to outline the possible problems and concluded his letter: 'However it is poor work pointing out difficulties.

I admire your pluck in facing them. I wish you heartily every success.'

There are no such quandaries about names and sex in the second story of the collection, 'A Case of Identity'. Unfortunately there is not very much at all that is of special interest. This is the weakest of the twelve tales, perhaps the weakest of the Holmes stories, as though Conan Doyle was taking a breath between two bouts of consummate storytelling.

Next came 'The Red-Headed League'. It is not hyperbole to say that this is one of the sharpest and most satisfying pieces of detective fiction ever written. In an effort to empty a shop adjacent to a bank a group of criminals devise a part-brilliant, part-hilarious, scheme to remove the red-headed owner of the shop from his business so that they can dig down into the bank below without being overheard. They establish the Red-Headed League and stage a competition with a lucrative prize to find to best head of red hair in the area. Of course they judge the shop owner, Jabez Wilson, as the champion and thus remove him from his business. Holmes solves all with some masterly detection, including at the beginning of the story the observation about Jabez Wilson that: 'Beyond the obvious facts that he has at some time done manual labour, that he takes snuff, that he is a Freemason, that he has been in China, and that he has done a considerable amount of writing lately, I can deduce nothing else.' The explanation? Wilson's right hand is larger than his left, he having worked with it and developed the muscles; he wears a Masonic symbol on his tie-pin; his right cuff is shiny for five inches; he has a tattoo on his wrist that is peculiarly Chinese and a Chinese coin on his watch-chain. Wilson's reply epitomizes the response that Conan Doyle, and Holmes, so despised. 'I thought at first you had done something clever, but I see that there was nothing in it after all.'

This reference to Freemasonry is not the only one made in the Holmes canon or in other works by Conan Doyle. He himself had become a Freemason in Portsmouth in Phoenix Lodge Number 257 but was never particularly active in the organization. Later attempts to link Freemasonry with Jack the Ripper and Arthur Conan Doyle are the stuff of sheer fantasy, the product of conspiracy theorists with too much time on their hands.

'The Boscombe Valley Mystery' began in the best Holmesian style. 'We were seated at breakfast one morning, my wife and I, when the maid brought in a telegram. It was from Sherlock Holmes, and ran in this way . . .' The story features former bandits from Australia, a train journey, Holmes searching for his clues with his lens, an innocent man cleared, a problem solved and Inspector Lestrade, the representative of the police establishment, made to feel acutely uncomfortable. Holmes also manages to free the guilty party because of extenuating circumstances, a feature of the Holmes stories that recurred in the works and became extremely popular with readers. It was Holmes playing Solomon, or God, making judgements about right and wrong, good and bad, that the courts and police were incapable of equalling. As such he was often above the law, just as he was above most of his fellow mortals.

'The Five Orange Pips' concerns the Ku Klux Klan and its evil ways and was perhaps inspired by the lynching of eleven Italians in New Orleans by a racist mob who believed them to be members of the Mafia. The federal authorities refused to intervene in the case and the Italian government withdrew its minister to Washington in protest.

'The Man with the Twisted Lip' is about a respectable journalist who discovers that he can make more money as a beggar than as a middle-class businessman. Action also takes place in an opium den, involves disguises and deception and also features a scene where Dr Watson's wife refers to him by the name of James instead of John. There are some evocatively drawn scenes, such as: 'But there was no difficulty in the first stage of my adventure. Upper Swandam Lane is a vile alley lurking behind the high wharves which line the north side of the river to the east of London Bridge. Between a slop shop, and a gin shop, approached by a steep flight of steps leading down to a black gap like the mouth of a cave, I found the den of which I was in search. Ordering my cab to wait, I passed down the steps, worn hollow in the centre by the ceaseless tread of drunken feet, and by the light of a flickering oil lamp above the door I found the latch and made my way into a long, low room, thick and heavy with the brown opium smoke, and terraced with wooden berths, like the forecastle of an emigrant group.'

The first collection of six short stories, written in a burst of intense activity, is a remarkable achievement. The second six, less hurried by financial necessity than the first group but again written extremely quickly, have also established themselves as miniature masterpieces. These stories appeared under a slightly different heading in the *Strand Magazine* and Conan Doyle himself was given a higher profile. He had written five of them by November and threatened, in a letter to his mother, to kill off Holmes in the final story. She persuaded him not to and instead influenced the background and plot for the twelfth tale, 'The Copper Beeches', in which an attractive young governess called Violet Hunter is obliged to cut off her red hair. The plot of this story is strongly gothic in nature and features insanity, hysteria and a bloody conclusion. Mary Doyle clearly knew the tastes of detective readers.

The story was preceded by five delicious tales. 'The Adventure of the Blue Carbuncle' was a Christmas story with Holmes once again providing some extra-legal judgement. A stolen jewel is hidden and then lost in a Christmas goose and Holmes uses his understanding of human nature, and of the meaning of Christmas, to solve the case and leave almost everybody satisfied. This was followed by one of the most famous stories in the Holmes canon, 'The Adventure of the Speckled Band'. A young woman is in trouble and after a night-long vigil, a tale of the

Indian past and a particularly intelligent snake, all goes well. Again, Sherlockians have troubled themselves with the appearances of snakes in the stories, wondering if Conan Doyle was subconsciously discussing the sexuality of Holmes or himself. He was more likely consciously discussing snakes.

In 'The Adventure of the Engineer's Thumb' Conan Doyle used his medical training to write about amputated limbs and Holmes uses his detective expertise to discover who did the amputating. Fellow Scotsman Robert Louis Stevenson, whom Conan Doyle never met, wrote to him to tell of how a native of Samoa reacted to the story. It was ironic praise.

'I am reposing after a somewhat severe experience upon which I think it my duty to report to you. Immediately after dinner this evening it occurred to me to re-narrate to my native overseer Simele your story of "The Engineer's Thumb". And, sir, I have done it. It was necessary, I need hardly say, to go somewhat farther afield than you have done. To explain (for instance) what a railway is, what a steam hammer, what a coach and horse, what coining, what a criminal, and what the police? I pass over other and no less necessary explanations. But I did actually succeed; and if you could have seen the drawn, anxious features and the bright, feverish eyes of Simele, you would have (for the moment at least) tasted glory. You might perhaps think that, were you come to Samoa, you might be introduced as the Author of "The Engineer's Thumb". Disabuse yourself. They do not know what it is to make up a story. "The Engineer's Thumb" (God forgive me) was narrated as a piece of actual factual history.'

The remaining two stories in the twelve tales were "The Adventure of the Noble Bachelor" and "The Adventure of the Beryl Coronet", both fine mysteries but neither of the first rank in the collection. The reviews of the short stories were generally very good, if less numerous than they deserved. The speed of the writing and of publication was so great that Conan Doyle was less interested in how his work was greeted than he might otherwise have been. It was harder to hurt him this time. The review of *The Adventures of Sherlock Holmes* in the December 1892 issue of *The Bookman* was by Joseph Bell, to whom the book had been dedicated. He was taken with Conan Doyle's writing and, not surprisingly, with the developing character of Sherlock Holmes. 'He has had the wit to devise excellent plots, interesting complications,' he wrote of his former student and of his work. 'He tells them in honest Saxon-English with directness and pith; and, above all his other merits, his stories are absolutely free from padding.'

This assessment was true and it was something of which Conan Doyle was always proud. He regarded himself not so much as an author but as a storyteller, able to capture and hold his readers' attention. He told friends, and foes, that the purpose of his work was not to produce any great, extended vision of change but to pursue the simple, pure and difficult task of telling a story well, lucidly and with the appropriate degree of pace. He told G.K. Chesterton that a good story, long or short, was all about rhythm[6] and that without a natural ability to control a story, tempered and refined with training, no writer could entertain people for very long.

One of the best insights into the first collection of Sherlock Holmes short stories, and into the entire canon, was written by T.S. Eliot later in Conan Doyle's life. He expressed what so many people had begun to feel, that Holmes had taken on a momentum and a reality that was now greater than the character's creator, and arguably greater than that of any other fictional personage. Yet when he is taken in parts, analysed and criticized, it is not immediately clear how this happens. 'It is of course the dramatic ability, rather than the pure detective ability, that does it,' wrote Eliot. 'But it is a dramatic ability applied with great cunning and concentration; it is not split about. The content of the story may be poor; but the form is nearly always perfect. We are so well worked up by the dramatic preparation that we accept the conclusion – even when, as in "The Red-Headed League", it is perfectly obvious from the beginning.' He continued: 'Every critic of The Novel who has a theory about the reality of characters in fiction, would do well to consider Holmes. There is no rich humanity, no deep and cunning psychology and knowledge of the human heart about him; he is obviously a formula. He has not the reality of any great character of Dickens or Thackeray or George Eliot or Meredith or Hardy; or Jane Austen or the Brontes or Virginia Woolf or James Joyce: yet, as I suggested, he is just as real to us as Falstaff or the Wellers. He is not even a very good detective. But I am not sure that Sir Arthur Conan Doyle is not one of the great dramatic authors of his age.'

The Conan Doyle family lived a relatively quiet life in South Norwood, managing to keep their feet dry from the literary fame splashing at their door, at least when they wanted to. A son, Alleyne Kingsley, was born in 1892, much to the joy of a father who had long wanted to teach his child to play cricket, to box and to aspire to those emphatically 'masculine virtues' of the triumphant late Victorian. As Conan Doyle approached the age of thirty-four he could take stock of a situation that could not have been predicted when he was a boy in Edinburgh, a struggling medical student or an unfulfilled doctor. He had travelled to Norway with Jerome K. Jerome and tried skiing for the first time; he had dined, drunk and joked with some of Britain's and Europe's finest writers; he was regarded by publishers and magazine editors as one of the most profitable authors of the time, and his financial and domestic affairs were more than satisfactory.

Conan Doyle's health was good but he was showing signs of a mild hypochondria. For the first time he was worrying about age, concerned that the runs around the football field and the late nights and early mornings were no longer so effortless and enjoyable. This was a time for young men, for fit men, he thought, and told friends that foreign belligerence and an unstable empire could lead to war. To be deprived of the great test of human character – war – by the fate of chronology, to be youthful and capable between rather than during conflict, was something he did not care to contemplate. Perhaps his little boy, this child in his arms, would one day raise his arms in anger against the enemies of his country. As a father he would be proud of that. Life, death, honour, courage. All of them seemed to find a resting-place in the thoughts and dreams of Conan Doyle.

He worked harder than ever. In 1892 Henry Irving bought a stage play about the Battle of Waterloo from him for £100. He also worked on an operetta, *Jane Annie*, with his friend J.M. Barrie. Short stories and essays were now being produced in larger numbers and the *Strand* told him that although it would publish as much of the material as it could, there was simply not enough space for all of Conan Doyle's work. Jerome K. Jerome's *The Idler* took some of the pieces, and other magazines also took his work. Friends advised him to slow down, worried that he might write himself out. Not at all, said Conan Doyle. They didn't know him well enough; nobody knew him well enough if they believed that.

Eighteen ninety-three was a harder year. In October Conan Doyle's father Charles, that unfortunate man who had found the world such a large, difficult place, died. Father and son had not got along when Conan Doyle was young but the relationship had improved in later years. No time now for further contact, not at least in this world. But there were the children and there was Louise. The couple visited Switzerland for a holiday, where both enjoyed the climbing and walking. Within weeks of her return, however, Louise began to sleep badly, was in some pain and developed a constant, painful cough.

'I had no suspicion of anything serious, but sent for

the nearest good physician,' wrote Conan Doyle. 'To my surprise and alarm he told me when he descended from the bedroom that the lungs were very gravely affected, that there was every sign of rapid consumption and that he thought the case a most serious one with little hope, considering her record and family history, of a permanent cure.' With two children, aged four and one, and a wife who was in such deadly danger, the situation looked almost impossible. Conan Doyle confirmed the diagnosis by calling Sir Douglas Powell down to see his wife, and then devoted all his energy and time to tackling the problem. 'The home was abandoned, the newly bought furniture was sold, and we made for Davos in the High Alps where there seemed the best chance of killing this accursed microbe which was rapidly eating out her vitals.'

Conan Doyle's medical training told him that his Touie was suffering from a disease that was invariably fatal. But submission was not an option. His stamina and determination were remarkable, even if his state of mind was dark and he sometimes wept to himself. It was as though he was pushing himself into an escapist world of work and planning so as not to think about what could, probably would, happen to his family in the coming months. Louise, on the other hand, was startlingly optimistic and courageous about it all, smiling when she could do so and trusting that if anyone could solve this bloody mess it was her husband, Arthur Conan Doyle. A disease is progressive, it exists, it has an end, hence it can be attacked, dealt with, defeated. He had taken on other adversaries, always won. This would be no different.

The family travelled to a valley in the Swiss Alps. They lived at the Kurhaus Hotel in Davos, the four of them, and tried their best to continue the happy family life they had until recently known. Conan Doyle read to Louise, performed mimes for her, slept by her side so as to be able to comfort her and get her whatever she wanted, whatever the time. He made her laugh, made the children laugh. And even made himself laugh. Or was his laughter a disguise? The sun was usually shining, the air was fine and smelt of a high freshness, a pure, cleansing wind. She looked a little better. Maybe she *was* a little better. Did she feel better? No, not quite yet. Give it time. He did. She was laughing at his jokes more now, amused by the mimicking of Jerome, Wilde, Chesterton – he pushed his stomach out for that one – and the other authors whom she knew or had met. Many of them wrote to her, and to him, passing on hopes and prayers. One night he thought he heard his father telling him that everything would be all right. Had Louise heard him? No, but she was sure that if Arthur had done so then the man must have spoken. There had to be hope.

There was. But it could never be long-term. Whether Conan Doyle had helped his wife we do not know but he was convinced that the trip abroad and the various precautions had worked miracles. Louise would live for another thirteen years. She was an invalid, often in bed, and sometimes attacks would endanger her life, but at least she was alive.

Conan Doyle's father was dead, his wife was dying. Death. It didn't seem to be fair. He was tired of so many things now, almost afraid that more pain would follow. Better that he be in control of it, that he chart its course. He had told his mother in April 1893: 'I am in the middle of the last Holmes story, after which the gentleman vanishes, never to reappear. I am weary of his name', and in his memoirs he wrote: 'I saw that I was in danger of having my hand forced, and of being entirely identified with what I regarded as a lower stratum of literary achievement. Therefore as a sign of my resolution I determined to end the life of my hero. The idea was in my mind when I went with my wife for a short holiday in Switzerland, in the course of which we saw the wonderful falls of Reichenbach, a terrible place, and one that I thought would make a worthy tomb for poor Sherlock.'

He joked that his bank account might die with his

detective but that he was still determined to make a clean break. He had been writing a further series of short stories, collected as *The Memoirs of Sherlock Holmes*, after being approached in February, 1892. The collection was to include 'Silver Blaze', 'The Musgrave Ritual', 'The Naval Treaty' and 'The Greek Interpreter'; the introduction of Sherlock's brother Mycroft; and, in the first story, that most quoted of Sherlockian comments about 'curious incidents'. The dog, the detective is told, did nothing at night. 'That,' says Holmes, 'was the curious incident.'

But of all of the stories it was the last, the twelfth, that caused the greatest reaction. 'The Adventure of the Final Problem' appeared in December 1893 and was supposed to end the career of Sherlock Holmes and liberate Conan Doyle from his man's embrace. That grip proved to be stronger than that applied by Holmes's enemy at the falls in Switzerland. Holmes and Moriarty – 'Ex-Professor Moriarty of mathematical celebrity . . . is the Napoleon of crime, Watson' – face and fight each other and Holmes ends his own life in removing the consummate criminal from the face of the earth.

When Watson arrives at the scene there is neither a detective nor a criminal. There is, however, a letter from Holmes to his old friend. 'I write these few lines through the courtesy of Mr Moriarty, who awaits my convenience for the final discussion of those questions which lie between us. He has been giving me a sketch of the methods by which he avoided the English police and kept himself informed of our movements. They certainly confirm the very high opinion which I had formed of his abilities. I am pleased to think that I shall be able to free society from any further effects of his presence, though I fear that it is at a cost which will give pain to my friends, and especially, my dear Watson, to you. I have already explained to you, however, that my career had in any case reached its crisis, and that no possible conclusion to it could be more congenial to me than this.' He concluded, 'Pray give my greetings to Mrs Watson, and believe me to be, my dear fellow, Very sincerely yours, Sherlock Holmes.'

The unimaginable. Holmes was dead, sacrificing his own life for the salvation of his fellows. Had the teachings of the Jesuits left their mark on Conan Doyle? The reaction, first in London and then in the rest of Britain and, later, the United States and Europe, was extraordinary. Conan Doyle had his reasons for doing such a thing and they were thoughtful, well argued and understandable. He wanted a fresh start, wanted to be taken seriously for writings other than Sherlock Holmes, desired to wash his hands of an earlier era that he now associated too readily with the death of his father and the terrible illness of his wife. But none of these motives was known to the reading public, to the men and women who had written to Sherlock Holmes, who assumed or wished him to be a real person, who had lived vicariously through his adventures and rushed to buy each new instalment of his life. To the partisans of Holmes more than a hero had been killed – a limb had been amputated.

In London young men wore crape bands around their hats, there were protests outside magazine offices and letters of complaint were sent to newspapers, Members of Parliament and even the Prince of Wales. Mourners marched in Fleet Street, some readers thought that it was all a huge practical joke and in New York there were complaints that a mock version of a Sherlock Holmes story had somehow been published which let the man die. It all seemed so strange to Conan Doyle, who was experiencing his own loss, more real and tangible and far more permanent than any of this. He even received threatening letters, evidence of that peculiar creature who even today is convinced that Conan Doyle is almost irrelevant to the process of placing Sherlock Holmes's life on the page. He told them to read the story properly, to read the final paragraphs and then to come to sensible conclusions.

Fittingly, they are the words of Watson, always loyal and usually more eloquent and wise than some might believe.

'A few words may suffice to tell the little that remains. An examination by experts leaves little doubt that a personal contest between the two men ended, as it could hardly fail to end in such a situation, in their reeling over, locked in each other's arms. Any attempt at recovering the bodies was absolutely hopeless, and there, deep down in that dreadful cauldron of swirling water and seething foam, will lie for all time the most dangerous criminal and the foremost champion of the law of their generation . . . As to the gang, it will be within the memory of the public how completely the evidence which Holmes had accumulated exposed their organisation, and how heavily the hand of the dead man weighed upon them. Of their terrible chief few details came out during the proceedings, and if I have now been compelled to make a clear statement of his career, it is due to those injudicious champions who have endeavoured to clear his memory by attacks upon him whom I shall ever regard as the best and the wisest man whom I have ever known.'

These final words are surely influenced by Plato on the demise of Socrates. 'Such was the end, Echecrates, of our friend, who was, as we may say, of all those of his time, whom we have ever known, the best and most righteous man.' The end of the wisest man. And birth for new wisdom.

4

To Defend What is Right

Travel had always rejuvenated Conan Doyle. He enjoyed the different assumptions and attitudes that he found abroad and the new challenges he encountered. He never altered his opinion of the superior nature of the British people but this was founded on a vision of duty rather than a philosophy of exploitation or racial difference. Even in sophisticated Europe he saw unfulfilled promise. Switzerland, Germany and Austria, he thought, lacked the British capacity for humour and self-mockery. Southern Europe needed to organize itself. North America he was less sure about. An opportunity to visit the United States and Canada came in 1894 and he asked his brother Innes, now a young subaltern, to accompany him. They crossed on a German liner and noticed with alarm the German hostility towards Britain and the British. During a party on the ship Conan Doyle noticed that various German and American flags had been hung; he promptly drew a Union Jack and placed it above its rivals.

Once they had docked in New York the first words Conan Doyle and his brother heard were 'Dr Conan Doyle, I presume?' They were met by Major J.B. Pond, a larger-than-life impresario who had fought in the American Civil War and, from what the writer could see, had been at the centre of almost every event of importance in

American history. Pond took Conan Doyle to several large meetings where the audience were eager to see, hear and meet the creator of Sherlock Holmes. He was not an especially impressive sight. Whereas other British authors, from Charles Dickens onwards, had dressed in ostentatious costumes or used theatrical devices, Conan Doyle merely presented himself. He was untidy, often forgetful about his dress and sometimes ill-prepared as a lecturer. He later wrote that he took some pride in his public speaking, and when he outlined his views on lecturing the judgement of those who knew him or had heard him was that they were touching, heartfelt but somewhat pathetic. Later he explained: 'I have my own theory of reading, which is that it should be made as natural and also as audible as possible. Such a presentment is, I am sure, the less tiring for an audience. Indeed I read to them exactly as in my boyhood I used to read to my mother. I gave extracts from recent British authors, including some work of my own and as I mixed up the grave and the gay I was able to keep them mildly entertained for an hour.'

Some of the local newspapers in the United States disagreed and found Conan Doyle to be disappointing and inadequate. Yet at his best he was popular and engaging. In Chicago, Indianapolis, Cincinnati, Toledo, Detroit and Milwaukee, he won friends and converts. He also crossed the border into Canada and spoke in Toronto. He would return to Canada and it was this country, with its Scottish foundation, British colonial link and rugged beauty, rather than the United States, that captured his heart. He spoke to 1500 people at Massey Hall and then went to Niagara for a sight seeing trip. He told his ailing wife that Niagara Falls and not those at Reichenbach should have been where Holmes and his enemy had met their deaths.

Generally the tour was a success in that it introduced Conan Doyle directly to tens of thousand of readers and potential readers, and indirectly to millions of them. Even in 1894 the book-buying market in the United States was

Arthur Conan Doyle with his father, Charles Doyle, 1865.

Below
His mother, Mary Doyle, 1891.

A Stonyhurst cricket group in 1873, with Conan Doyle on the right of the back row.

Connie, Lottie and Annette, Conan Doyle's sisters, in Lisbon.

Dr. Joseph Bell, Conan Doyle's professor and the man Sherlock Holmes was modelled on.

Sidney Paget, the man who illustrated the Sherlock Holmes
stories for *Strand* magazine, in 1891.

Bush Villa in Southsea, where the first Sherlock Holmes story was written.

Jean Leckie, later to become Conan Doyle's wife, 1896.

With the Branger brothers, 1894

With James Payn, who accepted Conan Doyle's first stories and later recommended him to someone else, 1897.

Conan Doyle in fancy dress as a Viking at Windlesham, 1898

In South Africa, 1900.

massive and ever growing. Yet this period of travel was not the cathartic, restful or enjoyable exercise that Conan Doyle had hoped for – which partly explains why he left for Egypt so quickly after returning to England. But first he purchased some land on which to build a house in Hindhead, Surrey, and hired one of his old friends from his Southsea days, Mr Ball, as architect. This in hand he set off for a land he had as yet only read about.

'Once at Cairo we took up our quarters at the Mena Hotel, in the very shadow of the Pyramids, and there we settled down for the winter . . . On the whole it was a pleasant winter and led up to a most unforeseen climax. I ascended the Great Pyramid once and was certainly never tempted to do so again, and was content to watch the struggles of the endless drove of tourists who attempted that uncomfortable and useless feat. There was golf of sorts and there was riding. I was still an immature horseman, but I felt that only practice would help me, so I set forth upon weird steeds provided by the livery stables opposite. As a rule they erred on the side of dulness, but I have a very vivid collection of one which restored the average. If my right eyelid droops somewhat over my eye it is not the result of philosophic brooding, but it is the doing of a black devil of a horse with a varminty head, slab-sided ribs and restless ears. I disliked the look of the beast, and at the moment I threw my leg over him he dashed off as if it were a race. Away we went across the desert, I with one foot in the stirrup, holding on as best I might. It is possible I could have kept on until he was weary, but he came suddenly on cultivated land and his forelegs sank in a moment over his fetlocks. The sudden stop threw me over his head, but I held on to the bridle, and he, pawing about with his front hoofs, struck me over the eye, and made a deep star-shaped wound which covered me with blood. I led him back and a pretty sight I presented as I appeared before the crowded verandah! Five stitches were needed, but I was thankful, for very easily I might have lost my sight.'

Egypt seen to be believed, and not to be seen again if Conan Doyle could help it, the author returned to his literary work. This period saw the publication of two books. The first, in 1896, was *The Exploits of Brigadier Gerard*, about a man who had fewer problems than his creator with matters equestrian. Conan Doyle had written about Gerard before, in short-story form, but now produced a full book about the French hero. Conan Doyle was less proud of his Gerard tales than of his other historical work, but he thought they had a place in the genre. The hero was based on the Baron de Marbot, who wrote a set of memoirs and was a vain, ostentatious man with a love of pomp and boasting but who also demonstrated great skill and courage in battle. Both *The Exploits* and, in 1903, *The Adventures of Brigadier Gerard*, were written for amusement and almost as rest in between what the author liked to consider as more serious and worthy work. He had read and written about Napoleonic matters for almost three years and Gerard materialized naturally and almost effortlessly. Ironically many critics at the time and a large number since have detected in the Gerard adventures many of the qualities lacking in Conan Doyle's other non-Sherlockian writing. He is comic without being ridiculous, absurd while still being believable and, at times, sympathetic and convincing. This was the only truly and consistently amusing character created by Conan Doyle and one that deserves to stand the test of time.

The second book of the period was *Rodney Stone*, published in 1896. The advance payment for this novel was one of the most lucrative Conan Doyle ever received, for a book which gave him an enjoyment and satisfaction hardly equalled in his literary career. Smith, Elder & Co paid him £4000 and the *Strand* paid a further £1500 for serial rights. The subject of the book was prizefighting during the Regency period. Conan Doyle's fascination with boxing was shared at the time by George Bernard Shaw, though Shaw never developed the right hook and defensive jab used by Conan Doyle. He had boxed at school, university and while on board ship and had got into the odd less-organized contest with a young man in Southsea. The sport appealed to Conan Doyle for many of the reasons that it repels others, then as now. He admired the isolated courage of the single, lone fighter in the ring with nothing with which to defend himself other than his strength, skill and nerve. This was the warrior model; the extension of that child who in the Edinburgh yard had thrown stones at his enemies, his back against a damp wall.

Conan Doyle was also knowledgeable about boxing. He attended tournaments and matches, writing to Israel Zangwill about the state of Jewish boxing in London. Zangwill told him that the number of rising young Jewish fighters was most encouraging, both for the sport and for the Jews. Conan Doyle also put his name to various committees of former public-school boys who as a measure of social reform and improvement were starting boxing clubs for the sons of the poor in London's East End and Glasgow. He once told a friend that if it had been possible he would much rather have made his living by his ability with his fists, holding a bat or kicking a ball than by wielding a pen.[1]

The plot of *Rodney Stone* is simple but inviting, even though Conan Doyle himself said that only a boxing connoisseur could appreciate all of the book. The story is told through the eyes of a boy who watches the achievements of Gentleman Jackson, Jim Belcher and Daniel Mendoza with relish and awe. 'I had always a weakness for the old fighting men and for the lore of the prize-ring, and I indulged it in this novel' Conan Doyle wrote.[2] 'At the time boxing had not gained the popular vogue which I have been told that this very book first initiated, and I can never forget the surprise of Sir George Newnes when he found out what the new serial was about. "Why that subject of all subjects upon earth?" he cried. However, I think that the readers of "The Strand" found that I had not chosen badly, and the book is one which has held a permanent place as a picture of those wild old days.' In fact Conan Doyle's book had little to do with the growing interest in boxing at the turn of the century – created by charismatic fighters from the United States and a change in the law – and friends who told him otherwise were evidently less than trustworthy critics.

But the book gave him joy. And joy was in short supply at that time as Conan Doyle's wife suffered ever more painful attacks and spent increasingly long periods in bed. She was an invalid now, unable to accompany her husband anywhere and seldom able to talk with him for very long. She had also been incapable of performing any sexual act for some time, and there is no reason to believe that before the attack of tuberculosis the couple enjoyed anything but a healthy sex life. Nor is there any evidence that after Louise became ill Conan Doyle conducted any affairs or frequented prostitutes. The morality of the era allowed, or at least accepted, the use of prostitutes, and extramarital relationships were known and tolerated in Conan Doyle's circle. It is safe to say that if he had gone elsewhere for sexual gratification few people would have condemned him. He was honest, sometimes brutally so, with his friends and confided in them to a sometimes dangerous and foolhardy degree but there is no evidence in letters, memoirs or contemporary observation that he betrayed his dying wife.

Home life was difficult but Conan Doyle did his best to sustain some form of normality. He would sit by Louise's bed and read to her from his work in progress, discuss reviews of his writings and chatter about their mutual friends and other authors. She was fond of Jerome K. Jerome and Conan Doyle made her laugh with stories of Jerome's efforts to keep his *Idler* solvent and with anecdotes about drinking sessions around the magazine. Sometimes Louise would fall asleep and it was only after Conan Doyle had finished his story that he noticed. He would help her to eat and drink, watch her wake and be ready to fetch anything she wanted, and make sure that she was never alone. Yet he was alone. Romantically and emotionally. Until 15 March 1897, when he met a young Scotswoman by the name of Jean Leckie.

They met at a party in London and this daughter of wealthy parents living in Blackheath had a delicious singing voice, rode a horse with professional skill and laughed sweetly, delicately, and often reminded Conan Doyle of how beautiful women could be. She was fourteen years his junior and used her relative youth with panache. She knew the man's writing and admired him: she thought that Sherlock Holmes was the creation of a genius and even compared the medieval tales to the best of Sir Walter Scott.

This was no passing infatuation, but something deep and, for Conan Doyle, unique. He had never felt these things for Louise, even before she had become ill. He told his mother that he had fallen in love with another woman and she accepted what had happened. He told close friends as well and they were divided on the subject. Some wondered why he was bothering to keep the affair platonic, while others thought his actions no better than sexual infidelity. None of it really mattered. He was in love. He would nurse, cherish and be faithful to Louise until the day he died, he told himself as well as Jean, even if she lived for another thirty years.

The hard work of literature always acted as an outlet of energy for Conan Doyle yet this period of sexual and emotional frustration was bitingly difficult. He was restless, often difficult and sometimes reacted foolishly and belligerently to criticism. He refused to resurrect Sherlock Holmes even though friends advised him that work on the detective might distract him from the pain of his personal life. There were short stories, there were lectures and there was an emerging spiritualism but this was still a relatively barren time. He looked abroad and to international politics to keep his mind away from what was happening at home. Conan Doyle was a passionate imperialist of the old school, unsure about some of the new ideas of economic control over the colonies and more attached to a less tangible, more romantic notion of a never-setting sun. This was an imperialism of optimism, of progress, of the notion of Britain extending, whether the colonized nations wanted it or not, democracy and parliamentary government. In particular he looked to development in South Africa.

Conan Doyle knew the country and he knew the people. Unlike many Britons during the 1890s he had a great respect for the Afrikaners, the Boers, for their rural toughness and hard independence. He had a great admiration for the Huguenots, those French Protestants who with the Dutch and to some extent the Germans, made up the Afrikaner people. He perceived some of the qualities of his beloved Scotland and its single-minded farmers in South Africa and its white tribe and even recognized some of what he thought were his on qualities in the Boers. But conflict was coming. The Boers and the British had been uneasy allies, mutually suspicious fellow-pioneers and now potential enemies. And if war came, as Conan Doyle was convinced it would, he must be there. There had been several colonial conflicts during his life, the most recent being in the Sudan. He had missed them all, and he was determined not to miss this one.

Conan Doyle was forty when the Boer War started in 1899 and although a fit man for his age he was more than thirty pounds overweight and a fine target for any Boer marksman in search of a well-known British author to pot. He offered his services to the army but was told that the war would be over quickly, that there were more than enough British and imperial troops of the right age and that, anyway, he would not be able to keep up with the rest of the men. He was hurt at being told that he was out of condition, angry that London should rely on colonial troops. On 18 December of that year he wrote to *The Times*: 'The suggestion comes from many quarters that more colonials should be sent to the seat of war. But how can we in honour permit our colonial fellow-civilians to fill the gap when none of our own civilians have gone to the front? Great Britain is full of men who can ride and shoot. Might I suggest that lists should at least be opened and the names of those taken who are ready to go if required – preference might be given to those men who can find their own horses? There are thousands of men riding after foxes or shooting pheasants who would gladly be useful to their country if it were made possible for them. This war has at least taught the lesson that it only needs a brave man and a modern rifle to make a soldier.'

He was referring in this last sentence not to the British soldiers in South Africa but to the Boers, farmers with little organized military training but with a skill with weapons, horses and camouflage learnt from childhood. Conan Doyle knew that this was an enemy fighting for home and family, not for some abstract idea of empire or philosophy. Shaken by the losses of British men and aware that his stories had a strong influence over many younger Britons, Conan Doyle volunteered to serve as a doctor in his friend John Langman's medical unit of fifty beds and as many men. Louise and his friends told him not to go but he insisted. There was something quixotic, typical of Conan Doyle, about the decision. He had argued in favour of the Boers to friends, explaining that these people had a perfect right to be angry and nervous at what had happened in the Transvaal. Gold had been discovered and Johannesburg immediately became home not only to law-abiding miners anxious to become rich but to criminals and peripatetic gangs of men who followed them. The leader of the Boers in the region, Paul Kruger, was not prepared to give these people an open house or full rights and imposed a heavy tax on them. This Conan Doyle understood, even applauded.

Matters became more complicated when Cecil Rhodes became Prime Minister of Cape Colony and helped a group of imperialist adventurers to attack Transvaal. The Jameson Raid failed and tension between the British and the Boers became almost tangible. The British troops in South Africa were supported by the people of Britain and, to a large extent, by the government; the Boers, seen as a plucky little people facing up to a mighty empire, were the darlings of Germany, Belgium and much of Europe. The two sides squared off. It was when Britain appeared to be being slandered by continental Europe that Conan Doyle placed all his support behind his country and its cause.

The war actually began when the Boers invaded South Africa and laid siege to Ladysmith, Kimberley and Mafeking. Things did not go well for Britain and her allies. Conan Doyle was not surprised. Always a keen and informed military historian and a passionate observer of the army, he knew that British tactics had not changed in decades. The British had, almost without exception, fought only native soldiers since the Crimean War, almost half a century earlier. Their method of movement and advance against the Russians had been Napoleonic in its form and look; it had failed in the Crimea, and it would be a disaster in Africa. It was. This was a new form of warfare. The Boers organized themselves into small, fast units of riflemen and could ride away from action back to their villages without being caught. When they attacked *en masse* they came on in what seemed like a disorganized manner but turned out to be successful and surprising. They reserved their fire, they used native tactics, they used the land. 'From December 10 to 17, 1899, was the black week for England,' wrote Conan Doyle. 'In that week General Gatacre lost a battle at Stormberg, Lord Methuen lost one at Magersfontein and General Buller lost one at Colenso. The three together would not have made more than a minor action in the great war to come, but at the time it seemed portentous.'[3]

Reaction in the British army was less slow than shocked. The 1890s were nothing if not comfortable for Britain, not yet exposed to the changes brought about by trouble in Ireland, the rise of the trade union movement, the campaign for women's suffrage and the inexorable expansion of

German military and economic power. These things were near in time but still far away in mind. All was fine, Britain was fine, Conan Doyle was fine. And now this. Britain's soldiers had far too few machine-guns for their numbers and their officers had still not formulated viable plans for their use. The reserve of ammunition was far too small and almost gone by the end of the first week's fighting, and there were not even enough uniforms for replacement men, the bulk of material for the army still being made in blue and red instead of the khaki necessary in the terrain of southern Africa. The experience of the soldiers ranged from the pathetic to the petrifying. Their boots were not made for the fiercer heat of the region and fell apart, men complaining that as they ran into battle they suddenly found that their stockinged feet were on the ground and that the soles of their boots had been left yards behind. There were far too few medical tents and supplies for the wounded, and men were obviously dying not from the effects of the enemy's bullets but from neglect.

Conan Doyle heard of all this in Britain, having close friends and contacts in the military. He wrote that men must put down their wine glasses and pick up their rifles if the health of the Empire was to be honoured. To this end, and refused permission to pick up a rifle, he lifted a surgical bag instead. He began interviewing candidates for the hospital party and there was no shortage of volunteers, though some of them were not of the quality Conan Doyle would have liked. 'When we were complete we were quite a good little unit, but our weakness was unfortunately at the head. Dr O'Callaghan had been a personal friend of Langman's and had thus got the senior billet, but he was in truth an excellent gynaecologist, which is a branch of the profession for which there seemed to be no immediate demand. He was a man too who had led a sedentary life and was not adapted, with all the will in the world, for the trying experience which lay before us. He realized this himself and returned to England after a short experience of South African conditions. We were compelled to have one military chief, as a bond with the War Office, and this proved to be one Major Drury, a most amusing Irishman . . . he was a very pleasant companion in civil life, but when it came to duties which needed tact and routine he was rather too Celtic in his methods, and this led to friction and occasional rows in which I had to sustain the point of view of Mr Langman. I have no doubt he thought me an insubordinate dog, and I thought him – well, he has passed away now, and I remember him best as a very amusing companion.'

Many other members of the party were much better qualified and more content to undertake this demanding mission. There was a fine doctor, Charles Gibbs, there were cooks and stewards, storekeepers and orderlies. This was a self-contained, dedicated unit and its most charismatic member was a man who had not practised medicine for a number of years and was known to almost all the young men he treated as the creator of Sherlock Holmes. It came as a surprise to these wounded soldiers, but as others testified, it also came as a welcome distraction from the conditions of a war that was being lost. Those conditions were worse than Conan Doyle had expected. He arrived at the African war zone at the beginning of April 1900 and was astounded by what he saw. There was terrible fever in Bloemfontein because the Boers had cleverly cut off the water supply to the city and forced the British to drink infected water. There were as many men dying of fever as of the result of an armed clash.

'The outbreak was a terrible one. It was softened down for public consumption and the press messages were heavily censored, but we lived in the midst of death – and death in its vilest, filthiest form. Our accommodation was for fifty patients, but 120 were precipitated upon us, and the floor was littered between the beds with sick and often dying men. Our linen and utensils were never calculated for such a number, and as the nature of the disease causes constant pollution, and this pollution of the most dangerous character and with the vilest effluvia, one can imagine how dreadful was the situation. The worst surgical ward after a battle would be a clean place compared to that pavilion. At one end was a stage with the scene set for "H.M.S. Pinafore". This was turned into latrines for those who could stagger so far. The rest did the best they could, and we did the best we could in turn . . . In the very worst of it two nursing sisters appeared among us, and never shall I forget what angels of light they appeared, or how they nursed those poor boys, swaddling them like babies and meeting every want with gentle courage. Thank God, they both came through safe.'

Conan Doyle's concern for what he saw was genuine and consistent. Everybody who served with him, as soldiers or doctors, remembered a selfless man who was often profoundly shocked by what he saw. It was less the dirt and the suffering that the sheer mess and disorganization that appalled him. This was not like the war he had studied, not like the battles depicted in his books. He never wavered from his admiration for the character, resolve and toughness of the ordinary British soldier but he also never became used to the short tempers, the pointless arguments, the pornographic jokes of a bored, frightened army. He saw men looting, saw men terrified and saw men exhibit a courage that, he thought, those who had not seen war could not hope to understand.

His regard for the private soldier extended to the officer corps, many of whose leaders he met. But just like their men, some of these generals were not quite the princes Conan Doyle had assumed them to be, when he met them at close quarters. Kitchener was distant and out of touch, Buller had stored supplies for himself in a city that was supposed to be near to starvation. As for the bureaucrats and staff officers who controlled the army from London, they were often fools. Conan Doyle had conceived various ideas to improve military performance, to modernize tactics and to apply a scientific methodology to the South African war. Some of his suggestions were callow if enthusiastic but others deserved consideration. 'I was practising how to turn a rifle into a howitzer. I fastened a large needle at the end of a thread to the back sight. When the gun pointed straight up in the air the needle swung down across the stock and I marked the spot. Then the idea was to tilt the gun slowly forward, making advances of 200, 400 and so on in the range, so that you had a dial marked on the stock and could always be letting the needle fall across the correct mark on the dial to drop the bullet within a certain distance.

'But the crux was to discover the exact ranges. To do this I went down to Frensham Pond and, standing among the reeds and tilting the gun very slightly forward, I pulled the trigger. The bullet very nearly fell upon my own head. I could not locate it, but I heard quite a loud thud. But what amazed me, and still amazes me, was the time it took. I counted fifty seconds on my watch between the discharge and the fall.' The vision of a slightly plump man firing bullets over his head by a pond in the early morning might seem bizarre but Conan Doyle was actually working with a promising idea, one to be developed in the coming years. This first experiment, however, did not run smoothly. A man who Conan Doyle thought might have been an artist suddenly ran towards him and asked if he wanted to know where the bullets were going. Conan Doyle replied that he did not. 'Then I can tell you, sir, for they have been dropping all round *me*.'

The plans were sent to the War Office but the reply was patronizing and, Conan Doyle came to believe, entirely typical of its archaic attitudes. 'With reference to your letter concerning an appliance for adapting rifles to high angle fire I am directed by the Secretary of State for War to inform you that he will not trouble you in the matter.' Conan Doyle took the reply to the war and amused his friends by showing it to them when things were going badly. London was not 'troubling' us in this matter, he would say.

By the summer of 1900 the British had restored part of the situation in South Africa and although the conflict lasted for another two years it was clear that overwhelming military and economic power would win in the end. But before the war was over the British had introduced concentration camps into Africa, there was talk of other atrocities and the popular image of the poor, battered Boer farmer had taken root all over the world. This appalled Conan Doyle, carrying with it as it did an implicit, although sometimes aggressively explicit, condemnation of the British forces' behaviour in the Boer War. His only reaction was to write about his experiences. *The War in South Africa: Its Cause and Conduct*, a pamphlet that cost sixpence, was translated into many languages and sold more than 300,000 copies in Britain alone within two months of its publication. Almost all of the money Conan Doyle earned from it he donated to pertinent causes, such as the Civilian Rifleman's Organisation, the Union Jack Club and the Chelsea Pensioners; and, in an effort towards reconciliation, to Boers who had fallen on hard times and to a scholarship fund at Edinburgh University for South African students.

'I read the foreign correspondent of *The Times*. In a single column there were accounts of meetings in all parts of Europe – notably one of some hundreds of Rhineland clergymen – protesting against our brutalities to our enemies. There followed a whole column of extracts from foreign papers, with grotesque descriptions of our barbarities. To any one who knew the easygoing British soldier or the character of his leaders the thing was unspeakably absurd; and yet, as I laid down the paper and thought the matter over, I could not but admit that these Continental people were acting under a generous and unselfish motive which was much to their credit. How could they help believing those things, and, believing them was it not their duty by meeting, by article, by any means, to denounce them? Could we accuse them of being credulous? Would we not be equally so if all our accounts of any transaction came from one side, and were supported by such journalists and, above all, such artists as lent their pens and pencils, whether venally or not, to the Boer cause? Of course we would.'

Conan Doyle knew that there were expensively pro-duced, scholarly volumes about the war in South Africa and that government papers and state reports were available, but none of these would be read by ordinary people, including those of Britain, who were beginning to wonder just what their army had got up to in the Boer War. He was convinced that 'a direct imperative call' had driven every other thought from his mind and he had to write the pamphlet. Its contents were partisan but far from hysterical; this was the stuff of patriotic journalism rather than naked propaganda. At no time did Conan Doyle pretend that the conditions in the concentration camps were satisfactory but he did defend the logic behind their use. Boer fighters would ride out, shoot dead some British infantrymen and then ride back to their homes, immediately assimilated into the civilian population. Should the British authorities tolerate this piecemeal slaughter of their men or try to do something about what was happening? The question was rhetorical. By isolating the women and children of a particular Afrikaner town or village the British denied hiding-places to their enemies. The enemy had chosen to fight in such a manner, behind, as it were, the skirts of their wives and mothers. The British were merely responding in the only way possible.

The camps should have been clean and should have included sufficient food and water, Conan Doyle went on to argue, but it was worth remembering that the British seldom had adequate food or supplies. This argument was not completely accurate but it was at least as authentic as the anti-British hyperbole being published in Germany and, to a lesser extent, the United States. Conan Doyle felt that the men he had known in Africa were being misrepresented and that the British government was not doing enough to combat this.

On other issues Conan Doyle's views were less soundly

based. The British had been accused of torturing their prisoners, of raping and looting and of using the notorious dum-dum bullet. This bullet was named after a military outpost in India and incorporated a soft nose so that it exploded when it hit its subject, destroying a human body and tending to smash the morale of the soldiers who saw the victim. Conan Doyle denied that any of this had happened. In fact the dum-dum bullet had been used, even though British soldiers found with any in their equipment were punished. Easily constructed, it was moreover difficult to detect by superior officers; and in any case some officers turned a blind eye to its use. As for rape, torture and looting, these were extremely rare and almost all cases discovered were harshly punished.

The Boers, on the other hand, tortured and often executed any black men they caught fighting for the British cause, treated British prisoners of war callously and attacked their enemies while protected by the cover of the white flag of surrender. Conan Doyle emphasizes that it was surprising that in some cases the British didn't act in a more uncivilized way. 'I made the comments as simple and as short as I could, while as to the accuracy of my facts, I may say that, save as to the exact number of farmhouses burned, I have never heard of one which has been seriously questioned,' he wrote. 'It was a glad day for me when I was able to lay down my pen with the feeling that my statement was as full and as effective as it was in me to make it.'

Others agreed. Soldiers, former soldiers and civilians stopped Conan Doyle in the street to shake his hand, street parties were held in Essex to congratulate the man, and an author and doctor took on the appearance of a national hero.[4] Conan Doyle was sufficiently balanced and stable never to let praise go to his head but he also knew when it was time to exploit his good fortune and strike out. He decided to suggest certain reforms of the army based on his experiences in the war. He had seen cavalry at work and it was practically useless.

Horses sometimes frightened native armies and the shock value of a charge certainly existed but against modern and well-armed soldiers the horse was now outdated. Conan Doyle had seen one lancer spear two Boers with one blow. He had also seen many horses killed underneath their British riders, the men slaughtered shortly afterwards; he had seen cavalry with side-arms dreadfully outgunned by Boer infantry and had seen the grotesque catastrophe of the organized charge and gallop against disciplined men with machine-guns. He also stressed the need for part-time reserves, militia or territorials. It took far too long, he argued, to train men from scratch and turn them into an organized army. A semi-trained militia who could by brief yet intensive training be transformed into regular standard troops was essential, especially as European armies could now call upon hundreds of thousands of soldiers and move them by train extremely quickly.

The army, as usual, did not treat the ideas very seriously but was obliged by popular opinion to at least acknowledge them and pay them lip-service. Most of them would be incorporated into British military practice before too long, though not quickly enough to avoid disasters in France and Belgium just over a decade later. Conan Doyle's disappointment was short-lived. At the beginning of April 1902 he was offered a knighthood by King Edward VII. It is a mark of the man's attitude that his first response was incredulity, followed by reflection and finally by a refusal to accept the award. Not for the likes of him, he thought. It was emphasized, however, that this was not for the creation of Sherlock Holmes but for his work for the British cause in the Boer War. Conan Doyle's mother, again a fount of advice for her son, urged him to accept. He said he would. Not for his services to the British cause but for his services to the British soldier.

5

The Real-Life Detective

During the Boer War and the years following it Conan Doyle became a public figure on a far greater scale than ever before. He was now known by people who had never read a Sherlock Holmes story and it was assumed that he would become more involved in public and political matters. Representatives of the two main political parties had approached him and asked for his support several times in the past and newspaper profiles had speculated about a political career. He carried himself well, was confident in public, was comfortable in crowds and believed in public service.

As for his politics, he was obviously not a radical, clearly believed in empire and, suspicious of the new and rising Germany, put his faith in a strong army and navy. He also thought that Liberal leader Henry Campbell-Bannerman – who once said that the best place from which to run a country was in bed – was a despicable man not to be trusted at all. Conan Doyle wanted to stand as an independent against Campbell-Bannerman in the latter's own seat but in the end had to settle for a contest in Edinburgh, which he fought as a Unionist. The 1900 'Khaki' General Election went well for Conan Doyle's party but not so well for him. Edinburgh was an impossible constituency for a Unionist and even though Conan Doyle performed well – far better than many had expected – he lost the seat. He took comfort in the fact that anti-Catholicism was a factor and that some of his opponents accused him of being a Jesuit spy or an unfrocked priest.

'The Radicals used to attend my meetings in great numbers, so that really, I think, they were often hostile audiences which I addressed. Since their own candidate held hardly any meetings I was the only fun to be had. Before the meeting the packed house would indulge in cries and counter-cries with rival songs and slogans, so that as I approached the building it sounded like feeding-time at the Zoo. My heart often sank within me as I listened to the uproar, and I would ask myself what on earth I meant by placing myself in such a position. Once on the platform, however, my fighting blood warmed up, and I did not quail before any clamour. It was all a great education for the future, though I did not realize it at the time, but followed blindly where some strange inward instinct led me on. What tired me most was the personal liberties taken by vulgar people, which is a very different thing from poor people, whom I usually find to be very delicate in their feelings.'

With his understanding of 'poor people' Conan Doyle would stand again for Parliament, but before then what about those poor people who had been deprived of Sherlock Holmes? He was still reluctant to resurrect Holmes but there was always the possibility of a story about the detective from earlier days. This, he thought, would enable him to write one last Sherlock Holmes tale but not to have to find an explanation for the reappearance of the man after his death in Europe. The idea for *The Hound of the Baskervilles* originated on a golfing holiday Conan Doyle had with Bertram Fletcher Robinson, the nephew of the editor of the *Daily News*, in Cromer, Norfolk in March 1901. Robinson, whom Conan Doyle had met on his way back from the South African war, told him during their holiday of an old country legend and the two men spent some hours discussing its possibilities and eventually agreed that Conan Doyle should write what many believe to be the best of the Sherlock Holmes stories. The two men then went to Dartmoor together and at this stage Robinson was deeply involved in the project. Conan Doyle even told his mother that 'Robinson and I are exploring the moor together over our Sherlock Holmes book'. After the story was published as a magazine serial and book and was such a success – the *Strand* published seven printings, the most in its history – Conan Doyle began to change the story of Robinson's involvement, eventually referring to it as a 'remark'.[1]

Nothing in Conan Doyle's life and career should make us think that he was dishonest or dishonourable and certainly not a plagiarist or fraud. The manuscript of the book is in Conan Doyle's own hand, though this proves nothing. At worst Conan Doyle purposely downplayed the contribution of his friend to *The Hound of the Baskervilles*; at best Robinson was merely a man with an interesting idea and a friend who could write superlative stories; the truth might lie somewhere in the middle. Whatever the complete truth – and we will never know it – the plot, pace, characterization and brilliance of the book are all undoubtedly vintage Conan Doyle.

The Hound of the Baskervilles is unique among the Holmes stories in that the story came first and Holmes was used merely as a heroic clothes-horse on which to hang a plot. Inevitably the detective grew to a coruscating brilliance in the book but Conan Doyle's original thought was simply to tell a story. This was not the rebirth of Sherlock Holmes, he told friends and critics who teased him for his lack of resolve in bringing back Holmes back to life. This was to be a story of the demon hound of Dartmoor. The tale of the devilish dog was published in the *Strand* between August 1901 and April 1902 (and as a book in 1902, straight after serialization) and the immediate reaction was extremely positive. Readers noticed a more intricate and sophisticated story with a successful flashback – some of the other tales are weakened by poor use of this device – and a stronger, more consistent tension.

Holmes and Watson travel to Dartmoor, near to Princetown Prison, to solve the case of the death of Sir Charles Baskerville. They are greeted by the dark, Gothic and overpowering Baskerville Hall, an escaped prisoner on the loose and a moor vomiting up clues, death and reminders of matters prehistoric. The writing is some of Conan Doyle's best, evocative and rich without being heavy-handed. 'The avenue opened into a broad expanse of turf, and the house lay before us. In the fading light I could see that the centre was a heavy block of building from which a porch projected. The whole front was draped in ivy, with a patch clipped bare here and there where a window or a coat-of-arms broke through the dark veil. From this central block rose the twin towers, ancient, crenellated, and pierced with many loopholes. To right and left of the turrets were more modern wings of black granite. A dull light shone through heavy mullioned windows, and from the high chimneys which rose from the steep, high-angled roof there sprang a single black column of smoke.

'"Welcome, Sir Henry! Welcome, to Baskerville Hall!"'

And welcome to the once and future Sherlock Holmes. The success of *The Hound of the Baskervilles* was so great that offers from London and New York for new Holmes stories reached Conan Doyle in their dozens. The amounts offered, especially from the United States, were enormous and Conan Doyle was finding it difficult to resist. His disinclination to write more about Holmes had also diminished. Perhaps it was time to bring the man back. Colliers in New York offered him $4000 for each story, of whatever length he thought fit. They wanted a minimum of six but as many as he could manage. An American setting or two would be helpful but, again, this was entirely up to the author. Conan Doyle gave in, signing a contract for eight stories with an option for four more.

But how to bring Holmes back? He had died at Reichenbach Falls – Watson knew it and Holmes had told him as much in a letter. But if Sherlock Holmes could decipher the past he could also predict, with relative certainty, the future. In the first of the new stories, 'The Adventure of the Empty House', Holmes suddenly confronts Dr Watson, who promptly faints. The explanation of Holmes's survival and reappearance is staggering in its audacity. After Watson has recovered from the first and only faint of his life he is told by Holmes that Moriarty died in the struggle and that he, Holmes, realized what a chance this was for complete victory. There were friends of the professor who would kill Holmes once they heard of their leader's death but who would be off guard if they thought that Holmes had also died in the struggle. This would give Holmes the chance to track them down and destroy them. 'I had thought this all out before Professor Moriarty had reached the bottom of the Reichenbach Falls.' Holmes also explains that he then climbed up the rock above the falls and hid so as to see Watson 'investigating in the most sympathetic and inefficient manner the circumstances of my death'. But Moriarty had not been alone. Holmes had to flee and since that time only his brother Mycroft knew that he was still alive.

The explanation reveals Holmes at his most resourceful and fertile, Watson at his most loyal and touching. The thought of the latter, solemn to the point of tears, searching for clues to the death of his closest friend, is both delightfully simple and profoundly moving. The plot of the story is a straightforward account of an assassin trying to murder Holmes and the detective's use of a dummy to deceive his enemy. There are better mysteries in the other stories but none so intimate in describing the relationship between Holmes and Watson.

Collier's magazine knew that this would be so when it announced the forthcoming series on 19 September 1903. 'In next week's issue of *Collier's*, the Household Number for

October, will begin the most notable series of short stories of the year – "The Return of Sherlock Holmes", by Sir A. Conan Doyle. Those familiar with the previous adventures of the famous detective – and are there any who are not? – will remember that the last heard of Mr Holmes was the report that he had been hurled headlong over a precipitous cliff. It was not believed that any man – either in fact or fiction – could survive such a shock as this, and even the detective's best friends (even those who most realised the very good reasons Holmes might have for wishing himself to be considered dead) began to give up hope of ever hearing of his wonderful genius or of witnessing its almost infallible operation. But Holmes did not die. He survived the deadly peril through which he passed, and of this and of the ensuing adventures Sir Conan Doyle tells us in the remarkable series which he has called "The Return of Sherlock Holmes".' The *Strand* published a similar advertisement and even distributed handbills announcing the return of the detective.

The other stories in the collection include some of the most popular and accomplished of the Holmes canon. 'The Adventure of the Dancing Men' is one of several Holmes stories that tackles the issues of adultery and of sexual affairs that take place before as well as during a marriage. Conan Doyle obliged his American publisher by using the United States as the background for this story and obliged readers by a clever use of an underworld cipher – the dancing man. 'The Adventure of Black Peter' appeared in early 1904 and was heavily influenced by Conan Doyle's days on a whaling ship. The violence in this story is particularly graphic and, once again, Holmes plays judge as well as detective. The first time we meet Holmes in this story he has a 'huge barb-headed spear tucked like an umbrella under his arm'. He explains to Watson: 'If you could have looked into Allardyce's back shop you would have seen a dead pig swung from a hook in the ceiling, and a gentleman in his shirt-sleeves furiously stabbing at it with this weapon. I was that energetic person, and I have satisfied myself that by no exertion of my strength can I transfix the pig with a single blow. Perhaps you would care to try?'

'The Adventure of Charles Augustus Milverton' presents one of Holmes's more intriguing and fascinating enemies, an accomplished and repugnant blackmailer. Milverton is eventually shot dead by one of his victims but not before Holmes and Watson have indulged in burglary. 'The Adventure of the Six Napoleons' was published in April 1904 and is one of the most enduring of the stories. A pearl is hidden and several busts of the French emperor are smashed, apparently for no reason. What is the connection? Holmes knows the answer. As he did in 'The Adventure of the Second Stain', where matters of state and world peace depend on his solving a mystery. He does, and in so doing comes into contact with a beautiful woman named Lady Hilda Trelawney Hope.

Conan Doyle was satisfied with the stories and with their reception and was now a wealthy man, able to accept or reject work at will. No amount of wealth could solve his domestic problems, though; Louise was clearly deteriorating and sometimes completely unable to talk or even open her eyes. The affair with Jean Leckie was stronger than ever, though still not sexual, and at his worst Conan Doyle despised himself for wishing for the death of his wife. These thoughts came in the dark hours when Louise was asleep and he thought of the emptiness of their time together. It had been thus for some years now and nobody even pretended that matters would get any better. He had nursed her as best he could and hardly ever lost patience; when he did he found it difficult to expunge the guilt and frustration from his mind. All was going so well with his literary career, and even with his social and sporting life – he had kept up his cricket, managing to take seven wickets for only fifty-one runs for the Marylebone Cricket Club against Cambridgeshire. But both writing and sport were only distractions from the reality of his situation.

Jean Leckie was supremely patient and spoke about Louise

only when Conan Doyle mentioned her deliberately in conversation, but there was still surely the chance that this attractive and desirable woman would finally have had enough. She could meet someone new, unattached and younger and Conan Doyle would be left with nothing but a dying wife and fond memories of what might have been. He sometimes asked Jean if she ever contemplated leaving him and added quickly that he would entirely understand. It was because he would entirely understand, she repled, that she loved him so much and could never leave him. He would return her smile and hold her hand.

Did Louise know about all this? She did. She too loved this good man and because of that would never have rebuked him or forced him to sit beside her bed night after night. She too thought about her coming death with feelings other than dread and fear because it would be a release for her husband as well as for her. Conan Doyle had considered divorce and had become involved in supporting new and progressive divorce laws, but he never seriously considered such a thing in his own life. More people all the time knew of his relationship with Jean Leckie and fewer minded. Conan Doyle and Jean did not care what they thought. They spoke about what married life would be like together, about going out as a couple and holding their heads high, about sleeping together, waking together.

Then, without warning, in the summer of 1906 there was a change in Louise's condition. There had been periods of relative recovery in the past but now there was a sudden and steady decline. It was July. A good July. A warm July. The greatest irony of all, it was 4 July, the day the bulk of a continent celebrated its independence. Lady Conan Doyle, Louise Hawkins, died at three o'clock that morning. She was forty-nine. Independence. And Arthur Conan Doyle, forty-seven and internationally famous, wept like a baby.

He had not loved her in many years, perhaps never loved her in the way he now loved Jean. But respect, warmth, affection and regard, these he felt in abundance. Louise was buried at Hindhead and after the funeral Conan Doyle received up to five hundred letters a day. How guilty he felt now. The letters sympathized with him. He didn't deserve it. He also began to feel ill, weak, generally in poor health. There were no medical problems – as a doctor he knew this – but he still experienced the symptoms of various physical complaints. He thought he just might deserve it. Jean disagreed. They were married on 18 September 1907. In his memoirs Conan Doyle described her as 'the younger daughter of a Blackheath family whom I had known for years, and who was a dear friend of my mother and sister. There are some things which one feels too intimately to be able to express, and I can only say that the years have passed without one shadow coming to mar even for a moment the sunshine of my Indian summer which now deepens into a golden autumn.'

During his life Conan Doyle was known, somewhat unfairly, as a collector of causes. Every year a different world opinion to change, some people said. This wasn't completely true. Conan Doyle was a man with a passion not only for what he perceived as natural justice and order but also for personal victory. Once convinced of a case he would do almost anything to make sure that it was won. It was this combination of a powerful moral vision and an indefatigable desire to win that made him such a difficult opponent. Some of his chosen campaigns were badly timed, ill-considered and, in some cases, bordered on the absurd. But most were not. He was at best a man of unwavering ethical certainty and strength, at worst nothing more harmful than an inexorable eccentric.

One of Conan Doyle's most enduring campaigns was for the reform of British divorce laws. He first became aware of the existing legislation during the latter stages of his first marriage and he was convinced that it was unfair and outdated. Contrary to what some of his enemies suggested, this was not because he had ever seriously considered leaving his wife but, typically of the man, because he saw an injustice being committed against a minority: women. Laws dating from the middle of the nineteenth century had made it possible for a man to obtain a divorce on extremely flimsy grounds, including the alleged infidelity of his wife. A woman, by contrast, faced a terrible struggle if she wanted a divorce, usually having to prove a combination of extreme unfaithfulness and physical abuse by her husband. As men were allowed in law to 'chastise' their wives as a means of punishment, physical abuse had to be systematic and consistently brutal if it were to be cited in a divorce case. Divorce was also extremely expensive and because of the inheritance and property laws of the time few women had the resources to bring a divorce case to the courts, let alone win.

Conan Doyle had been approached by several reform groups asking for his support in changing a variety of laws, including those on divorce. He had resisted most of these demands, reluctant to become involved in issues with which he did not feel completely comfortable. But in 1906 Thomas Hardy, with whom Conan Doyle had become friendly during the past two years, formed a new society for promoting change in the divorce laws and invited a number of lawyers, writers and other public figures to join him. Conan Doyle was approached to join, accepted, and became passionately involved. Before long he was made president of the society and used all his influence as an author and a friend of the powerful to try to improve the situation. He had been owed some favours by a group of Conservative politicians since the Boer War and now he tried to take payment in the form of divorce law amendment.

In his memoirs he wrote: 'I am quite alive to all the arguments of our opponents, and quite understand that laxity in the marriage tie is an evil, but I cannot understand why England should lag behind every other Protestant country in the world, and even behind Scotland, so that unions that are obviously disgusting and degrading are maintained in this country while they can be dissolved in our Colonies or abroad. As to morality I cannot, I fear, admit that our morality here is in the least better than in Scandinavia, Holland or Germany, where they have more rational laws. I think that in some States in America they have pushed Divorce to an extreme, but even in America I should say that married happiness and morality generally are quite as high as with us. The House of Lords has shown itself to be more liberal in this matter than the Commons, possibly because the latter have a fear of organised Church influence in their constituencies. It is one of several questions which makes me not sorry to see Labour, with its larger outlook, in power for a time in this country. Our marriage laws, our land laws, the cheapening of justice and many other things have long called out for reform, and if the old parties will not do it then we must seek some new one which will.'

This was an extraordinary statement for a man with conservative views, even written as it was in 1923, long after Conan Doyle's days as an active politician. He was prepared to give his support to the Labour Party because it was more progressive on divorce and land laws even though he disagreed with the fundamental economic and social policies presented in its manifesto and detested the pacifism that so many of its leaders had advocated both in the Boer War and in 1914. After he wrote this, several of his Conservative friends questioned his motives and his wisdom. Did he realize, they asked, just how popular and influential he was in Britain? His support for a political party could help their chances substantially and, in the case of the Labour Party, would give them the increased credibility and respectability so important to their cause. Conan Doyle replied that party was nothing, consistent politics everything. It was up to the other parties to change their policy so as to accommodate him, not for him to trim his position so as to please them. Nobody was absolutely sure whether he was mocking his critics or not. He probably wasn't.

Throughout his life Conan Doyle received letters and visits from women who were living in dreadful relationships or who were, in his own words, 'on the run' from violent husbands. He never wavered in his support for these women and their cause. He was fierce on the issue and prepared to face opponents from all sides. The radical suffragettes despised him because of his opposition to votes for women both in 1906 and later. He was the victim of hate mail, had sulphuric acid poured through his letter-box and was booed at the theatre and at public events for a two-month period during a suffragette campaign against him. These women thought that his reforms were merely cosmetic, disguising the real issues and his desire to maintain the *status quo* and keep women in what they saw as a subservient position. An enemy on the vital question of female suffrage, they argued, could not suddenly become an ally in the fight to change the divorce laws. It was something that Conan Doyle could never quite understand and that always caused him concern.

From the opposite position the Church of England denounced Conan Doyle as an interferer without Christian beliefs who did not understand the basic moral and religious necessity of the existing divorce laws, crucial to the maintenance of the institution of marriage. He smiled at all this, aware that opponents of spiritualism in the Anglican church would pounce on any opportunity to condemn him. Once again organized religion had shown its true colours and its true attitudes, he said.

In 1912 Conan Doyle devoted his attention to what he saw as a libellous and gratuitous attack on the memory and reputation of the captain and sailors who had been aboard the *Titanic* on its final, fatal trip, in which over 1500 lives were lost. Nobody had doubted the courage and honour of the men who had tried their best to save the passengers, sent the women and children to safety first and risked and in many cases given their own lives so that others might survive. Indeed some newspapers almost celebrated the disaster as a national triumph. It was all too much for George Bernard Shaw. In May, in the *Daily News*, he wrote that the whole *Titanic* incident had been distorted by the press, that Captain Smith was an incompetent rather than a hero, that the ship had too few lifeboats and that rather than being an example of British grit and determination the sinking was a national scandal. The claims that the band played on so as to calm the crowd were nonsense, he claimed, and it was in fact just a way to keep the third-class passengers on the ship while it sank. His accusations went on.

Conan Doyle was outraged and thought that Shaw's attitude was shameful. How could he attack men who were unable to defend themselves and how dare this Irish outsider cast doubt on the Britain that Conan Doyle knew and loved so well? The two men debated the issue in print and on a public platform, and although Conan Doyle was sincere, thorough and consistent, it was Shaw who seemed to win the day, at least in the minds of the intelligentsia. As for the working and middle classes, Conan Doyle had long been and would long remain their champion in almost everything. His best moment was in a letter to the *Daily News* published on 20 May 1912.

'I have just been reading the article by Mr Bernard Shaw upon the loss of the *Titanic*, which appeared in your issue of May 14th. It is written professedly in the interests of truth, and accuses every one around him of lying. Yet I can never remember any production which contained so much that was false within the same compass. How a man could write with such looseness and levity of such an event at such a time passes all comprehension.

'Let us take a few of the points. Mr Shaw wishes – in order to support his perverse thesis, that there was no heroism – to quote figures to show that the women were not given priority in escape. He picks out therefore one single boat, the smallest of all, which was launched and directed under peculiar circumstances, which are now matter for inquiry. Because there were ten men and two women in this boat, therefore there was no heroism or chivalry; and all talk about it is affectation. Yet Mr Shaw knows as well as I know that if he had taken the very next boat he would have been obliged to admit that there were 65 women out of 70 occupants, and that in nearly all the boats navigation was made difficult by the want of men to do the rowing. Therefore, in order to give a false impression, he had deliberately singled out one boat; although he could not but be aware that it entirely misrepresented the general situation. Is this decent controversy, and has the writer any cause to accuse his contemporaries of misstatement?

'His next paragraph is devoted to the attempt to besmirch the conduct of Capt. Smith. He does it by his favourite method of "suggestio falsi" – the false suggestion being that the sympathy shown by the public for Capt. Smith took the shape of condoning Capt. Smith's navigation. Now everyone – including Mr Bernard Shaw – knows perfectly well that no defence has ever been made of the risk which was run, and that the sympathy was at the spectacle of an old and honoured sailor who has made one terrible mistake, and who deliberately gave his life in reparation, discarding his lifebelt, working to the last for those whom he had unwillingly injured, and finally swimming with a child to a boat into which he himself refused to enter. This is the fact, and Mr Shaw's assertion that the wreck was hailed as a "triumph of British navigation" only shows – what surely needed no showing – that a phrase stands for more than truth with Mr Shaw. The same remark applies to his "wrote of him as they would hardly write of Nelson." If Mr Shaw will show me the work of any responsible journalist in which Capt. Smith is written of in the terms of Nelson, I will gladly send a £100 to the Fabian Society.

'Mr Shaw's next suggestion – all the more poisonous because it is not put into so many words – is that the officers did not do their duty. If his vague words mean anything they can only mean this. He quotes as if it were a crime the words of Lowe to Mr Ismay when he interfered with his boat. I could not imagine a finer example of an officer doing his duty than that a subordinate should dare to speak thus to the managing director of the Line when he thought that he was impeding his life-saving work. The sixth officer went down with the captain, so I presume that even Mr Shaw could not ask him to do more. Of the other officers I have never heard or read any cause for criticism. Mr Shaw finds some cause for offence in the fact that one of them discharged his revolver in order to intimidate some foreign immigrants who threatened to rush the boats. The fact and the assertion that these passengers were foreigners came from several eye-witnesses. Does Mr Shaw think that it should have been suppressed? If not what is he scolding about?

'Finally, Mr Shaw tries to defile the beautiful incident of the band by alleging that it was the result of orders issued to avert panic. But if it were, how does that detract either from the wisdom of the orders or from the heroism of the musicians? It was right to avert panic, and it was wonderful that men could be found to do it in such a way.

'As to the general accusation that the occasion has been used for the glorification of British qualities, we should indeed be a lost people if we did not honour courage and discipline when we see it in its highest form. That our sympathies extend beyond ourselves is shown by the fact that the conduct of the American male passengers, and very particularly of the much abused millionaires, has been as warmly eulogised as any single feature in the whole wonderful epic.

'But surely it is a pitiful sight to see a man of undoubted genius using his gifts in order to misrepresent and decry his own people, regardless of the fact that his words must add to the grief of those who have already had more than enough to bear.'

It was a brave letter and won Conan Doyle the respect if not the approval of George Bernard Shaw. Shaw was heard to say that his detractor simply did not understand.

Strangely enough this was precisely what Conan Doyle had said about him.

If it wasn't matters as profound and important as divorce laws or the moral and maritime reputation of a nation it was galleries, the future of the zoo, the need for a new international language, care of the roads, photography, the Loch Ness monster. The man attracted causes whether he liked it or not. One was his campaign to improve the organization of British sports. Conan Doyle had equated sporting success with national character ever since his first games of rugby and football as a boy in Scotland, so he quickly accepted a request by Lord Northcliffe in 1912 to help organize the British Olympic effort and place athletics on a less cavalier footing. However, Northcliffe's enthusiasm for change did not last long and Conan Doyle was soon left with the whole enterprise. The British Olympic Committee was at loggerheads with Northcliffe, the press were angry at the British Olympic Committee and Northcliffe would trust only his own newspapers, and then only 'up to a point'. It took a large degree of diplomacy for Conan Doyle to salvage anything from the mess but he managed to convince the warring parties that if Britain was to assemble, manage and finance a team for the next Olympic Games everybody concerned had to put their disagreements aside and help to raise money and hire staff. An unstable peace did come about and a disappointing £7000 was raised for the next Olympic Games, to be held in Berlin in 1916. The money was spent elsewhere.

There is no doubt that Conan Doyle was at times exploited by cynical activists, anxious to use his name and reputation but he usually knew and respected the dividing line between optimism and naivety. He gave his name and help quite readily but he was invariably proved correct. He recorded a touching little incident that occurred to him while he was staying in London and walking along the Embankment. It is charming both because of its content and because he saw no reason why he shouldn't write it

This picture was used as Conan Doyle's official election portrait in 1904, but was actually taken three years earlier.

'Touie', Lady Conan Doyle, who died in 1906.

Windlesham, 1911.

Conan Doyle sitting in the Viking chair in the music room at
Windlesham, 1912.

Lilly Loder-Symons, 1915.

Conan Doyle and his sons, 1916.

With his children and friends on the beach at Eastbourne, 1916.

Eille Norwood and Conan Doyle at the Stoll Films Convention Dinner at the Trocadero Ballroom, 1921.

Harry Houdini surrounded by Conan Doyle and his family on the beach below the Ambassador Hotel in Atlantic City, 1922. This was shortly before Lady Conan Doyle received a 'spirit message' from Houdini's mother.

Kingsley, Conan Doyle's son, aged eighteen.

Crossing the Atlantic to New York with Lady Conan Doyle, 1923.

Conan Doyle shortly before his death.

His grave in the garden at Windlesham.

down for his contemporaries and future generations to see. As he was taking the fresh air beside the Thames 'a man passed me, walking very rapidly and muttering in an incoherent way. He gave me an impression of desperation and I quickened my pace and followed him. With a rush he sprang up on the parapet and seemed to be about to throw himself into the river. I was just in time to catch his knees and to pull him down. He struggled hard to get up, but I put my arm through his and led him across the road. There I reasoned with him and examined into the cause of his troubles. He had had some domestic quarrel, I believe, but his main worry was his business, which was that of a baker. He seemed a respectable man and the case seemed genuine, so I calmed him down, gave him such immediate help as I could, and made him promise to return home and to keep in touch with me afterwards.'

At this point we are being told of a classic swindle, a perfect example of a fool and his money losing sight of each other remarkably quickly. And then, without any secondary motive or doubts, Conan Doyle completes the story with, 'When the excitement was over, I had grave doubts as to whether I had not been the victim of a clever swindler. I was considerably relieved, therefore, to get a letter a few days later, giving name and address, and obviously genuine. I lost sight of the case after that.'

Conan Doyle stood a second time for the Unionist cause, in the seat of Hawick, Selkirk and Galashiels at the General Election. Once again he failed to be elected. He also tried his hand at another non-Sherlockian book and *Sir Nigel* was published in 1906. Conan Doyle thought that the book 'represents in my opinion my high-water mark in literature, and though that mark may be on sand, still an author knows its comparative position to the others. It received no particular recognition from critics or public, which was, I admit, a disappointment to me. In England versatility is looked upon with distrust. You may write ballad tunes or you may write grand opera, but it cannot be admitted that the same man may be master of the whole musical range and do either with equal success.'

But there were other tasks, other matters and problems to settle now. Conan Doyle received myriad letters from members of the public and even from police officers from all over the world, asking for help in solving criminal mysteries, dealing with incidents of injustice or even saving their marriages. He felt unqualified to advise on the last but in some cases did involve himself in what he thought were clear miscarriages of justice. The case of a man called George Edalji came to his notice through the newspaper *The Umpire* in 1906. The man in question had been arrested three years earlier in the West Midlands for the arcane crime of maiming cattle. Edalji was a curious character, isolated and something of a natural victim. His father was Indian and also a Church of England minister. The Reverend Shapurji Edalji had experienced some mild racism since taking over as vicar of Great Wyrley, Staffordshire, in December 1875, but nothing that had been particularly worrying. In 1888, however, he began to receive threatening, insulting and obscene letters. Eventually a servant admitted to having written them and the matter appeared to end there. But in 1892 and for the following three years further letters arrived, more violent in nature, obviously written by a different person. Similar letters were written to the Reverend Edalji's neighbours as well. As the quantity of letters increased other incidents occurred around the wretched cleric. Other clergymen received nasty or eccentric postcards, ostensibly signed and written by Edalji; graffiti was written on the wall of his home and the church, and rubbish was thrown on his front lawn. One particularly unpleasant letter to various prominent Anglicans alleged that Edalji had committed rape and adultery and that the writer of the letter could prove this. The police were hardly sophisticated in their approach, echoing one of the less flattering portrayals of the pedestrian Lestrade in the Sherlock Holmes stories.

They came to the conclusion that the culprit was and always had been the vicar's son, George Edalji. As soon as they made their suspicions known the letters, threats and rumours stopped. It seemed that they had found their man and halted a crime in one swoop.

Some years later, in 1903, local farmers in and near to Reverend Edalji's parish found their animals morbidly slaughtered. Sixteen horses, cattle and sheep had been killed, their stomachs cruelly cut open and their entrails left to hang. Immediately this happened another round of letters, to the police and to local dignitaries, accused George Edalji, now working as a lawyer in Birmingham, of having committed the crime. Basing their suspicions on the earlier letters apparently written by Edalji, the police arrested him and made a thorough search of his home. They did not have to search very hard. In easy reach were a pair of boots covered with mud, a damp and stained coat and trousers and, most damaging of all, four marked, dirty razors. When the police surgeons examined Edalji's clothes they found bloodstains and hair. Another expert, this time on handwriting, stated that the letters accusing Edalji of the mutilation were, in fact, written by Edalji himself. There could be no doubt of the man's crime, it seemed, but perhaps some question as to his sanity. He was prosecuted, found guilty and sentenced to seven years in prison.

It did not take very long for racism to give the case an even more unhappy face. Local newspapers and Birmingham magazines accused Edalji of being a strange pagan, though they did not know of what variety, and of having sacrificed good British animals to an alien, devilish god. Edalji's Christianity and his father's ministry did not alter matters for the press or for local opinion, which grew to almost hysterical proportions. It might have been thought that when similar atrocities on local animals continued during Edalji's imprisonment some doubts might have been raised about his guilt and eccentric theological practices. But no.

The rationale offered was that this evil man obviously had friends and allies, that the cult had a greater and more dangerous following than had been previously assumed and that more Edaljis, not fewer, should be more arrested. Even when someone confessed to having disembowelled his horse on the night that the attacks occurred the case remained closed. He caught the next ship to South Africa and claimed that the confession had been forced out of him by a brutal police.

There were, of course, some people who thought that the entire enterprise was ridiculous and that, more importantly, there had been a severe miscarriage of justice. A group of solicitors who had looked into the case compiled a petition and sent it to the Home Office. Nothing was done. But less than halfway through his prison sentence George Edalji was suddenly released, without any valid explanation. He was a free man but an unemployed one. He could not return to the law, having been found guilty of a major crime and lost his reputation. It did not require very much persuasion for an already suspicious town to condemn a clever young half-caste. More than this, the case had been so well publicized and Edalji's name was so uncommon that he would now find it difficult to build any sort of life for himself. There was nothing for it but to fight to clear his name. He began in a publication called *Truth*, which had also championed him while he had been in prison. As other newspapers took up the story the Edalji case began to be something of a talking point.

When the facts were stated clearly they were at best doubtful and at worst made no sense at all. How could any court have convicted this man? First, he had an alibi for much of the evening in question, for he had visited his bootmaker. Second, his father was prepared to provide an alibi for the rest of the evening. The ties of blood obviously made this a less dependable defence but commentators noted that Edalji the elder had an incomparable record of ethical behaviour and honesty and those who knew him thought he would not lie even for his son. Third, the mud that had been found on Edalji's clothing and boots was not like that in the field where the unfortunate horse had been slaughtered. Fourth, the razors were marked not with blood but with rust. Fifth, the police had been fundamentally incompetent and slapdash with the evidence and had clearly confused different parts of clothing. This simply was not acceptable.

'As I read, the unmistakable accent of truth forced itself upon my attention and I realised that I was in the presence of an appalling tragedy,' wrote Conan Doyle, 'and that I was called upon to do what I could to set it right. I got other papers on the case, studied the original trial, went up to Staffordshire and saw the family, went over the scene of the crimes and finally wrote a series of articles in the *Daily Telegraph* . . . As I bargained that they should be non-copyright they were largely transferred to other papers, sold for a penny at street-curbs and generally had a very wide circulation, so that England soon rang with the wrongs of George Edalji.'[2]

Conan Doyle may have been slightly exaggerating but the effect of his call for justice certainly had an effect. Those who rejected his point of view argued that this was not the world of Sherlock Holmes and that criminals and the police were something Conan Doyle did not really understand. They also said that this was the man who had other opinions about other real-life crimes, such as the infamous Jack the Ripper. He thought that the culprit might have dressed himself as a midwife and thus gone unnoticed through the streets of the East End of London because it was expected that a midwife would rush from house to house covered in blood, carrying a surgical bag. He even went a step further, opining that the murderer could be a woman. This Jill-the-Ripper hypothesis had caused Conan Doyle more than a little embarrassment, even though it is at least as plausible as the other suggested explanations of this still unsolved crime.

Mockery and disagreement did not matter. The hunt was on. Conan Doyle devoted himself to the Edalji story now, writing to friends for support and lecturing to packed halls about the shame of the country in treating this man so badly. He assured those who would listen that the case was becoming a national disgrace on an international stage and that the French were enjoying mocking the failure of British justice and policing. This was probably not true but it did have the desired effect. He took sympathizers to the scene of the crime and took them by the arm to the house, the church, the field, the farm. They climbed fences, threw themselves flat on the ground to examine the tiniest of details, searched corners for clues and evidence. This was Sherlock Holmes alive, a time of catharsis and sheer fun for Conan Doyle. He had not felt as young and energetic in years, he said, and was determined to be proved correct. It was a pleasure to start the day now and to be at the nerve-centre of this effort to see justice done.

'These wrongs would have been almost comic had they not had so tragic an upshot,' wrote Conan Doyle. 'If the whole land had been raked, I do not think that it would have been possible to find a man who was so unlikely, and indeed so incapable, of committing such actions. He was of irreproachable character. Nothing in his life had ever been urged against him. His old schoolmaster with years of experience testified to his mild and tractable disposition. He had served his time with a Birmingham solicitor, who gave him the highest references. He had never shown traits of cruelty. He was so devoted to his work that he had won the highest honours in the legal classes, and he had already at the age of twenty-seven written a book upon Railway Law. Finally, he was a total abstainer, and so blind that he was unable to recognise any one at the distance of six yards. It was clear that the inherent improbability of such a man committing a long succession of bloody and brutal crimes was so great that it could only be met by the suggestion of insanity. There had never, however, been any indication even of eccentricity in George Edalji. On the contrary, his statements of defence were measured and rational, and he had come through a series of experiences which might well have unhinged a weaker intellect.'[3]

Yet if Edalji had not committed the crime, who had? More to the point, who would do such a thing and try to blame this innocuous individual? Lack of motive, lack of opportunity and good character would not, it seems, be enough. Conan Doyle looked to Walsall Grammar School, near to the Edaljis' home and to a young man named Greatorex who had been there – the key to the school had been placed outside Edalji's home during his persecution. From this man he expanded his investigations to include one Rodney Sharp, named by a former headmaster of the school. Only days after Sharp's name was mentioned Conan Doyle received an anonymous letter claiming that the ex-headmaster was a liar and a cheat. The solution to the crime seemed to be taking shape.

Conan Doyle had several letters in his possession now and examined them for patterns of vocabulary and writing style. There had clearly been two different people writing letters in the period between 1892 and 1895, with totally different writing styles and vastly separate and distinct levels of education. Whenever the most likely culprit was considered Rodney Sharp's name refused to go away. Sharp had left the area in 1895 and worked in a butcher's shop. He left this trade to serve in the merchant navy and had experience with cattle from his time on board a cattle boat in 1902.

The authorities were now more humiliated than enlightened. It seemed that the more Conan Doyle discovered about the case the less likely they were to initiate another investigation, let alone stage a second trial. However, a government committee was eventually formed, consisting of Sir Albert de Rutzen, Sir Arthur Wilson and the Hon. John Lloyd. 'Their finding, which came to hand in June, was a compromise document,' wrote Conan Doyle, 'for though they were severe upon the condemnation of Edalji and saw no evidence which associated him with the crime, they still clung to the theory that he had written the anonymous letters, that he had therefore been himself contributory to the miscarriage of justice, and that for this reason all compensation for his long period of suffering should be denied him.'

It shook Conan Doyle's faith in a system he had defended for so long. Somebody was lying, somebody was covering up the truth and somebody was willing to let a good and innocent man's name be blackened rather than risk embarrassment by showing contrition and stating the facts. He described it as 'a wretched decision' and made his feelings known in public. He had expected better, he said, from a system, a class and a profession that was supposedly admired throughout the world. There were, however, positive results from all this. In time the Court of Criminal Appeal would be established and there is no doubt that Conan Doyle and the Edalji case influenced this. The Law Society also decided to readmit Edalji, which was an implicit statement of his innocence. Conan Doyle and the *Daily Telegraph*, which had followed the case and supported Edalji after his defender's original article, established a subscription fund which eventually raised more than £300. It was an indication of Edalji's character that one of the first things he did was to pay back an aged relative who had contributed to his defence costs. A fitting conclusion to the story is that George Edalji was invited to and attended the reception for Conan Doyle's wedding to Jean Leckie in 1907. 'There was no guest whom I was prouder to see,' the author wrote later.

Real-life detection was more appealing than Conan Doyle had ever imagined. This was the addition of flesh, blood, struggle and success to the character he had created on paper. After the Edalji case he received so many letters from the allegedly wronged that he had to employ a full-time secretary simply to reply to them. One case that came to his attention was luscious, in that it involved someone who was well acquainted with the underworld, and was in fact a member of it. 'In one respect the Oscar Slater case was not so serious as the Edalji one, because Slater was not a very desirable member of society,' he wrote. 'He had never, so far as is known, been in trouble as a criminal, but he was gambler and adventurer of uncertain morals and dubious ways – a German Jew by extraction, living under an alias.

Shortly before Christmas 1908 a helpless old woman named Miss Gilchrist was savagely beaten to death and her Glasgow flat robbed of some private papers and a valuable diamond brooch. The woman's servant, Helen Lambie, was out of the flat at the time of the crime, at a local shop for just a few minutes buying a newspaper. The murder had been noisy and the people living in the flat beneath Miss Gilchrist had gone to see what was happening. Unfortunately the witness, Mr Adams, had forgotten to take his glasses with him and could only testify to seeing a well-dressed man leaving the flat.

The local police knew that Oscar Slater had recently moved to Glasgow and was living with a Frenchwoman not very far from where the murder took place. Scotland Yard had told the Glasgow constabulary of Slater and had emphasized that although they had not been able to charge or convict him of anything they were confident that he was an active criminal.[4] After the police had published a description of a man they wanted to interview regarding the Gilchrist murder – medium height, perhaps five foot six inches, of dark complexion and wearing a grey coat and a cap – a fourteen-year-old girl called Mary Barrowman came forward and told the police that she had seen a man, almost run into him, leaving the scene of the crime. Her description differed from the previous one given: this time it was a young man around six feet tall and wearing a fawn hat – not a cap at all but a round hat.

Just a few days later it was discovered that Oscar Slater, officially working as a diamond-cutter, had pawned a diamond brooch and was now on his way to the United States. The fact that the brooch had been sold almost a month before the murder was either unknown to the police or, more likely, of little interest to them. They wanted Slater and Slater they would get. He and his girlfriend had sailed for New York on 26 December on the *Lusitania*. The Glasgow police cabled New York and told the authorities to detain Oscar Slater. Now an extradition order was needed and this required reasonable evidence of a potential conviction and a strong possibility of guilt. Three so-called witnesses to the murder were shown photographs of Slater and after enjoying a free ride to New York confirmed that he was indeed the murderer. Matters seemed at an end when a small hammer was found in the man's possession, and his protests that it was necessary for his work in the diamond trade were ignored. On his return to Glasgow Slater was marched before an identity parade that consisted almost entirely of police detectives. Ironically, he had returned to Britain quite readily, confident that the only way to establish his innocence was to do so in the open. Experienced in the ways of the police, this usually self-possessed man began to wonder if he was going to come out of all this mess alive.

Conan Doyle thought that the whole business was preposterous but also realized that 'the public had lost its head, and so had the police. If the case had completely gone to pieces surely it could be reconstructed in some fresh form. Slater was poor and friendless. He had lived with a woman, which shocked Scotch morality. As one writer boldly said in the press: "Even if he did not do it, he deserved to be condemned anyhow." A case was made up in the most absurd manner . . . No attempt was ever made to show that Slater had any connection with Miss Gilchrist, or with the maid, Lambie, and as Slater was really a stranger in Glasgow, it was impossible to see how he could have known anything about the retired old maid. But he was not too well defended, while Mr Ure, the Advocate-General of Scotland, prosecuting for the State, thundered away in a most violent speech in which several statements were made, uncorrected by Judge Guthrie, which were very inexact, and which must have powerfully swayed the jury. Finally, the Crown got a conviction by nine votes to six (five "not proven") – which, of course, would have meant a new trial in England, and the wretched foreigner was condemned to death. The Scaffold was actually erected, and it was only two mornings before his execution that the order came which prevented a judicial murder. As it was, the man became a convict . . .' It was only a petition of more than 20,000 names which prevented the hanging from taking place.

Conan Doyle omitted to say that the case reflected a nasty, malodorous example of early-twentieth-century British anti-Semitism. Tens of thousands of Jews had arrived from Poland and the Ukraine between 1890 and 1905, during several massive pogroms. They had settled mainly in the heart of London's East End, but had also travelled to Manchester, Leeds, Glasgow and wherever they could find a home and work. There was even talk in Parliament of these newcomers storing coal in their baths and bringing either filthy diseases, revolutionary socialism or grasping capitalism into the land.

Even some British Jews – often of Sephardic origin, some of whom had been in the country for two centuries or more – who enjoyed assimilation and relative acceptance, were uneasy with this new mass immigration of Ashkenazim Jews which they thought would damage their position in society. A new community with few language skills, no political or economic clout and little knowledge of the workings of the British system and way of life, was an easy target for racism, ignorance or sheer police incompetence. When some Jews drifted into crime, as some members of most immigrant groups sometimes do – indeed as some members of most groups in general sometimes do – the cheap press exploited every possibility and every moment.

Conan Doyle was sympathetic to the Jews, was asked by Jewish friends to try to do something about the Slater case and, most important of all, he could not resist supporting the underdog whatever bark he or she had. But this case lasted a great deal longer than the Edalji lunacy. Slater was in prison for sixteen years before Conan Doyle managed to provoke some second thoughts on the verdict, in spite of the fact that alternative witnesses and even policemen had by then come forward to contradict some of the evidence that had convicted Slater in the first place. Slater managed to send a message to Conan Doyle through a friend of the alleged murderer just released from the same prison. This was just what Conan Doyle needed – a confirmation that even after so many years in prison Slater was still adamant that he was innocent. Drawing on the lessons learnt from the Edalji campaign, Conan Doyle contacted his friends in the press, held a conference on the Slater case and gave public speeches. A journalist in Glasgow, William Park, decided that the story was worth pursuing and as soon as he had reopened it the national newspapers in London, Edinburgh and Manchester followed hard behind.

Suddenly Glasgow was alive with English-accented reporters, all wanting to know about an incident that happened long ago and had been forgotten by most of the locals. The witnesses Helen Lambie and Mary Barrowman were found and interviewed and both admitted that they had accepted bribes, of £40 and £100 respectively, to place the blame on Slater. Lambie also revealed that Miss Gilchrist was not quite the delicate spinster that she had been painted and that she frequently received unusual visitors at late hours. Lambie had also, she said, been told to leave the house by Miss Gilchrist on that fateful evening. The police case fell apart within weeks of this new information and then Slater, not unlike Edalji, was suddenly released after eighteen years in prison for good conduct. No apology was ever made and the paths of Conan Doyle and Slater were not to cross again. It had been a victory of a kind. In a letter to the *Spectator* in October 1912 he wrote, almost wearily: 'some of us still retain an old-fashioned prejudice in favour of a man being punished for the crime that he is tried for, and not for the morals of his private life'. Some people certainly did.

6

A Crime Exposed

In 1909 Conan Doyle was fifty years old. He was slowing down now and had lost some of that zest for new adventure that had carried him almost effortlessly through his earlier years. Although he was still fit and healthy, the late nights of writing and the sheer quantity of letters of thanks, letters of refusal, letters of support had taken their toll. The balance between Conan Doyle the writer and Conan Doyle the public figure had swung too much to the latter for his liking and Jean told him that a new wave of people were under the impression that the author of the Sherlock Holmes stories was dead and that Sir Arthur Conan Doyle was a politician or an orator or something of that sort. This made him laugh, but not quite as much as he would have liked.

Two years earlier he had written *Through the Magic Door*, a collection of earlier essays and articles about writers who had inspired him. These included Edgar Allen Poe, Sir Walter Scott, Carlyle, Macaulay and the American historian Francis Parkman. It was interesting as an insight into the influences on him as a writer but it was not an original piece of work. His mind was elsewhere. It seemed that Africa was calling again, the continent that had fascinated him since childhood and had left an indelible mark since the Boer War. He kept a map of Africa on his study wall and followed the progress of the European empires, the evolution of new nations and the internecine and tribal wars of the region. Yet this was no myopic colonizer who thought that Europeans had the right, even the duty, to do as they saw fit in Africa and to use the peoples of Africa as slave labour and political pawns. He had watched and read about events in the Congo for some time now, with an increasing concern. King Leopold II of the Belgians had employed H.M. Stanley to be his agent in Africa and by the mid-1880s it was obvious that Belgium was intent on competing with its European rivals in the area and establishing a large colony there. Portugal and France immediately objected, the former pointing out that it was Portuguese explorers who had discovered the Congo, the latter merely sending in soldiers, builders and politicians. An international conference settled the problem by creating the Congo Free State, an enormous country with a European population of just 254 people, almost a fifth of whom were Belgian nationals.

These people owed their allegiance not to Belgium as such but to that nation's monarch, who was chief of state of the African country. The Belgian parliament had acknowledged that the 'union between Belgium and the new state of the Congo shall be exclusively personal'. Britain, France, Portugal and the United States were persuaded to take a minimal interest in the region and all the king's men spent a decade fighting the Arab slave traders who had been active in the region. Apart from geographical expansion it was the Congo's ivory and rubber that Leopold II wanted so dearly. The new overlords from Brussels might have beaten and expelled the slavers from the north but they ruled their plantations and 'their' black workers in conditions just as appalling, often worse. This was not the British way, suzerains in surrounding colonies began to say; this was uncivilized. It is ironic that the notion of relative ill-treatment should have been so prevalent but in the context of the period it should come as no surprise.

The British empire in Africa was exploitative but not unintelligent. Even the rawest imperialist who was interested in little other than national glory and national gain realized that cruelty towards the indigenous population was not only unethical but plain bad politics and planning. These people were not the only Englishmen who travelled to the empire. For every plantation owner, regional military commander or gentleman farmer there was a suburban doctor willing to spend a decade in a hill station as the only non-native, in treacherous conditions, with the sole purpose of treating medical problems that had not been cared for in centuries. He might be joined a hundred miles away by an Anglican or Methodist minister. Together they would bring an alien religion to Africa but also literacy, modern medicine and improved farming techniques so as to avoid periodic hunger and starvation. If these people were wicked exploiters they hid their baseness quite well. Conan Doyle knew many of them, was on committees to help them, had seen them in action.

This was not what was happening in the Belgian domain of the Congo. Rumours began to circulate in Westminster and before long rumours became factual reports. That imperialist of imperialists Joseph Chamberlain stated that natives from Sierra Leone had been treated terribly when they went to the Congo to work on a railway project. The reports were more than worrying. Africans were being whipped as they worked, men were killed or worked to death, women were being raped and children were being taken from their families. Any sign of rebellion or complaint was met with fists, feet and rifle butts and there was no attempt to provide anything resembling a safe workplace or decent food and drink.

The British consul in Boma, Roger Casement, actively opposed what was going on in the Belgian territory and assembled a group to work towards ending such mistreatment. In spite of his wife's advice and his agent and publisher's lectures, Conan Doyle decided that he had to get involved in what was going in the Congo. 'I examined this evidence carefully before I accepted it, and I assured myself that it was supported by five British consuls and by Lord Cromer, as well as by travellers of many races, Belgian, French, American, Swedish and others,' he wrote later. 'An attempt has been made since to minimise the facts and to pretend that Roger Casement had been at the back of the agitation for sinister purposes of his own. This contention is quite untenable and the evidence for the atrocities is overwhelming and from many sources, the Belgians themselves being among the best witnesses. I put in some two years working with Mr Morel and occasionally lecturing in the country upon this question, and it was certainly the efforts of the Congo Association which we represented, that eventually brought the question to the notice of that noble man King Albert which meant setting it right so that the colony is now, so far as I know, very well managed.'

The Congo Association was actually the Congo Reform Association, E.D. Morel was a shipping agent with a conscience and Roger Casement, who would come into contact with Conan Doyle later on, was an able administrator whose homosexuality and Irish nationalism smashed his once spotless reputation during the First World War. Conan Doyle does not do himself justice on this matter because it was by no means a simple exercise. The British Parliament gave its full support to opposition to the Congo atrocities and asked the national powers of the world to support it and offer suggestions. Ironically it was only Turkey who replied to the plea, an embarrassment to the reformers because Turkey's record of treatment of its conquered nations was as bad as that of the Belgian colonists. Leopold II rejoiced in the Turkish entry into the affray but was also worried by Britain's stand and by the failure of any major country to come to his support. He set up a committee to investigate the allegations but as soon as its composition was announced critics knew that no censure or condemnation would result. Eventually the Belgian king gave responsibility for the Congo to his parliament, who were so grateful for the gift that they almost considered passing a resolution calling for a republic.

Conan Doyle had had enough. While European politicians played at empire people were being treated, and killed, like animals. In eight days he wrote *The Crime of the Congo*, a 45,000-word indictment of the situation. He slept less than four hours a night, kept a jug of black coffee by his desk and ate packs of dry biscuits to keep up his strength. He drank Scotch at the beginning of this marathon but soon realized that it reduced rather than increased his work rate. He gave himself a daily word quota and, if he ever fell behind, stayed up until dawn to compensate. Some of his most productive times, he told friends, were as the sun showed itself and the whole world seemed to have gone away, leaving him alone with his pen and his thoughts. It was a supreme, splendid isolation. Jean was worried about his health through all this and thought that if he did not rest more often he would begin to hallucinate. He replied that it was under such conditions that the muse rested longest on his shoulder. He received and asked for no payment whatsoever for the booklet.

When *The Crime of the Congo* was published in 1909 it received international approval. The illustrations showed natives with their hands cut off, while the text gave detailed facts and figures about what had happened in recent years in the country. Figures as diverse as President Theodore Roosevelt, Mark Twain and Hilaire Belloc wrote letters of congratulations and support but also wondered what could be done and how. Pressure, replied Conan Doyle. Make the Belgian colonists feel pressure from governments, media and other colonies in Africa. But international politics was involved here and the Congo shared a border with German East Africa. Maybe so, he said, but there were under 3000 Europeans in all of the Congo, just over half of them Belgian. It could not be so difficult to make them listen to sense, with an emphasis on the word 'make'. He was being somewhat naive here, judging these men by the standards of the British settlements. Whereas the British wanted long-term colonies and believed in a concept of permanent empire, the Belgian colonists were eager only for a quick profit and a rapid return to their home country.

Eventually the situation did improve, partly due to Conan Doyle and his allies but also because of a change in administration in Belgium and the build-up to the First World War. Conan Doyle had few friends in high places as a result of his Congo work, though many supporters in low ones, but the central point is that he did not care. Although to modern sensibilities his ideas, beliefs and morals might seem archaic, we cannot, must not, judge him via anachronism. In his day he was a champion of social justice as he saw it, was viscerally opposed to injustice and cruelty and was never in any way intimidated by threats or by the possibility of repercussions and consequences. G.K. Chesterton thought that these qualities gave him a saintly quality and others believed that it proved that he was naive. In some way he was naive; he *wanted* to believe the best, was often shocked by the worst but never hid from it and let it be tolerated.[1]

These were happy years at home. A son, Denis, was born in 1909; another, Adrian, the following year and a daughter, Lena Jean, in 1912. In addition, Conan Doyle's growing fame was providing him with more opportunities to visit countries, attend events, experience a life new and fresh to him. The opening of a new railway line, the launching of a ship, the introduction of a new piece of technology into a major factory – all were assumed to be the sorts of thing Conan Doyle might be interested in and like to be invited to. He was made a patron of several new and developing sports and asked to participate in or observe some older ones. Lord's cricket ground was open to him at his will, and London rugby and football teams were happy to greet him as a privileged guest and to introduce him to their players. He revelled in it, relishing the company of sportsmen and their recollections of past triumphs. He was also instrumental in developing various sports, both in Britain and abroad. 'I can claim,' he wrote, 'to have been the first to introduce skis into the Grisons division of Switzerland, or at least to demonstrate their practical utility as a means of getting across in winter from one valley to another.' The claim was largely justified in that Conan Doyle brought Norwegian skis and skiing methods into Switzerland and brought about a change in Swiss attitudes towards skiing.

He was also asked to put his name to various new products, including soap, tobacco, newspapers, cars and even primitive fitness machines that were in fact completely useless. He rejected all such offers, even though some of them were lucrative, but rather enjoyed being asked. With the positive, even amusing side of fame came the problems of recognition. He did not mind requests for autographs and being pestered by the public but was genuinely disturbed by a series of death threats that occurred between 1910 and 1914. Conan Doyle's respect for courage was genuine in that he was himself a brave man; but he soon came to realize that however valiant he himself might be, his public utterances were liable to endanger his family. His comments about statements on Ireland, the suffragettes, individual criminal stories, Germany and the Russian socialists won him organized enemies. But there were also the ordinary cranks who thought that it might be a good idea to shoot or bomb a famous person. He tried to ignore most of his threatening mail but in early 1912 matters became so bad that he was given a police bodyguard. Nobody was ever charged with the threats and after 1918 the wave of intimidation simply stopped.

He was too busy at his writing as well to be too concerned with matters beyond his control. In 1912 he published *The Lost World* and gave the world another striking hero, Professor Challenger. Here was Conan Doyle's finest, most believable and accomplished character since Sherlock Holmes. There is also autobiography in Challenger, a man who reflected many of his creator's own beliefs and attitudes and, to a certain extent, his appearance. In fact Challenger is part Conan Doyle and part Conan Doyle's former teacher in Edinburgh, William Rutherford. 'He sat in a rotating chair behind a broad table, which was covered with books, maps, and diagrams. As I entered, his seat spun round to face me. His appearance made me gasp. I was prepared for something strange, but not for so overpowering a personality as this. It was his size which took one's breath away – his size and his imposing presence. His head was enormous, the largest I have ever seen upon a human being. I am sure that his top-hat, had I ventured to don it, would have slipped over me entirely and rested on my shoulders. He had the face and beard which I associate with an Assyrian bull; the former florid, the latter so black as almost to have a suspicion of blue, spade-shaped and rippling down over his chest. The hair was peculiar, plastered down in front in a long, curving wisp over the massive forehead. The eyes were blue-grey under great black tufts, very clear, very critical, and very masterful. A huge spread of shoulders and a chest like a barrel were the other parts of him which appeared above the table, save for two enormous hands covered with long black hair. This and a bellowing, roaring, rumbling voice made up my first impression of the notorious Professor Challenger.'

Like the Holmes stories, *The Lost World* is so written as to emphasize the hero's greatness. Edward Malone, the journalist who described him and travels with him on his adventures, is a Watsonian figure, seeing little wrong in his man and in awe of most of his achievements. The other characters in the story are mere shadows in comparison: a patrician hunter named Lord John Roxton and an elderly professor named Summerlee. Together the four travel to South America, where they find a group of dinosaurs which have somehow survived into the modern world. The book's setting and background are cleverly established and the apparently throw-away but in fact carefully prepared references to scientific discoveries, anthropological theories and biological history give the story a reality not found in all of Conan Doyle's writings. He knew this material from his medical training and from his general interest in the field and made good and convincing use of it here. There is also a female character in *The Lost World* – one who is more than a literary device or merely a necessary but incidental addition. Gladys is not the sort of woman with whom Conan Doyle felt acutely comfortable but he nevertheless paints a sympathetic portrait of her. She is independent, with spirit, intellect and great beauty. 'That delicately bronzed skin, almost Oriental in colouring, that raven hair, the large liquid eyes, the full but exquisite lips – all the stigmata of passion were there.' The stigmata of passion. Conan Doyle was on form once again.

The book's plot may have been outlandish and the Brazil featured in it may have been a country that had not existed for a very long time but none of this mars the story. It was a great popular success and gave its author much satisfaction. So much so that he wrote another Challenger story, *The Poison Belt*, which was published the following year. The story here is of the world apparently being enveloped in a deadly gas that seems to kill everything in its path. With the first approach of the gas people begin to act oddly and then, as time passes, drop to the ground. Challenger and his friends make a room completely airtight and wait for the gas to pass. When they emerge they find a terrible scene of bodies and mayhem. But as they watch, Challenger and his group of survivors realize that these seemingly dead people are getting to their feet and doing what they did before as if the gas had not come at all. They had been victims of a form of catalepsy.

Again, the book was a success and was read by some as a metaphor for preparation for a coming crisis. Conan Doyle was not alone in warning of the German attempt to build a navy and an army capable of taking on the world and winning. Britain's maritime dominance had been challenged and partly beaten. These were not the stable, safe and confident days of the 1880s and Conan Doyle was not the optimist he had been. He was unnerved by the complacency he saw around him in Britain. Worse, he was growing tired of his own country.

In 1914 the *Cornhill Magazine* offered him a trip to Canada and, to a lesser extent, the United States, to write a travel article and an account of a part of the empire unknown to most British people. He has also been invited by the Canadian government to tour the National Reserve at Jasper Park in the Rockies. He and Jean left their young family with friends, departed from Southampton on Wednesday 20 May on the SS *Olympic* of the White Star line and arrived in New York a week later. Conan Doyle was as much if not more of a celebrity in North America than he was in Britain. Immediately he set foot in New York he was both in demand and in trouble. He was asked by a scrum of journalists, who were already well aware of his views about female suffrage and smelt a good story, what he thought about women receiving the vote. The *New York Times* reported 'Sir Arthur replied that he thought the patience of the English public had been tried to the straining point by the actions of the militant suffragettes, and he would not be surprised at any time to hear that some of them had fallen victims to mob law. The police have had great difficulty protecting these women from the mobs on several occasions, he said.

'"Thus far," Sir Arthur went on, "public opinion, which usually guides the Government in England, has not demanded the entire suppression of the militant suffragette. It has almost come to that stage now, however, and something drastic will happen, and happen soon. There will be a wholesale lynching bee, I fancy, for the English mob, when thoroughly aroused, is not a respecter of sex. If anything happens the militants will only have themselves to blame."'

Other newspapers were less controlled. 'Sir A. Conan Doyle Fears Lynching for Militants,' said the *New York Evening Star*, 'Doyle Fears Lynch Law for Militants,' screamed the *New York Tribune* and, best of all, the *New York World* announced that 'Sherlock's Here; Expects Lynching of Wild Women'. It was an interesting start. Conan Doyle had left an England shaken by arson, physical attacks and disruption by radical women battling for the vote and he was never a man who was easily convinced of the righteousness of radicalism or the acceptability of political violence. Even so, he was outraged at the way some American journalists distorted what he had said, even claiming that he had offered to help the mob to lynch any suffragette they got their hands on. Anyone who knew Conan Doyle or anything of him would have realized just how out of character such a comment and an opinion would have been. Always savvy to the power of the press, and genuinely fond of the best journalists, he arranged an interview with Louis Sherwin of the *New York Globe*. He stressed that inaccurate reporting is 'perfectly monstrous' and then caused something of a laugh when he added, 'Why, some of my best friends are suffragettes.' He went on to dismiss the accusations that he had called for violence. 'And it isn't the least use denying it now – nobody will pay any attention to the denial. I thought of writing to the *Journal* about it – but what's the use? . . . you can never overtake a lie, particularly when it has twenty-four hours start. But it puts me in a most uncomfortable position – makes it appear that I am coming over here to say things I should not dare at home.'

One of the other crises in Britain was in 'John Bull's other island', where the situation was almost unmanageable. It was inevitable that a New York newspaper would ask about Ireland, and the *Times* obliged. Conan Doyle was candid and perceptive. 'Ulster will certainly fight but I do not expect any trouble there until they try to enforce the act. I do not believe there will be any small outbreaks, but if anything does happen, it will be serious. I tell you those men are not 'bluffing' as you term it. They mean business up there in the North of Ireland . . . In my opinion, it will be so serious as to amount practically to civil war, or it will be nothing at all. The men of Ulster will never give in to the idea of an Irish Parliament. I'm a Home Ruler myself, but I am certain there will be violence if there is any attempt to enforce the Home Rule Law.'

Conan Doyle's time in New York was crammed with visits, lectures and interviews. His energy and stamina were impressive and the American press told him so. He was only fifty-five, he protested, and joked that the best years of his life had not even begun yet. Even so, from 28 May until 1 June he was used to the full. On Thursday, the day after he arrived, he went on a tour of New York's skyscrapers, visited the Tombs prison, met some of the city's leading detectives and was the guest of honour at the Dinner of the Pilgrims at the Whitehall Club. He then went to the theatre to see John Drew and Ethel Barrymore in *A Scrap of Paper*. On Friday he went to City Hall and met the mayor. This was followed by a private dinner. The next day there was a trip to Sing Sing prison and then a baseball game between New York and the Philadelphia Athletics. Sunday offered a lecture and lunch, followed by a visit to Coney Island and the local police station. On Monday, the day before he left, he paid his respects at the funeral of John L. Griffiths, former United States consul in London, then a lecture and finally the opening of the Plaza Summer Garden and Air Terrace. At all these events he was expected to speak to the press, answer long questions, be available and friendly to the public and, most important of all, to not drop his guard.

On Wednesday 3 June he arrived in Montreal and in a country where he felt comfortable and welcome. Unusually among British writers of his generation, Conan Doyle preferred Canada to the United States. On this trip he also visited Winnipeg, Edmonton, Algonquin Park, Ottawa and Niagara Falls. This was his second trip to Canada and he was to visit the country once again, when he would grow to understand its complexities as well as its beauty. On this visit he was delighted by the natural beauty of the provincial parks and the sprawling wonder of the west, with its blossoming cities. But some of his comments lacked the insight that he usually showed.

'I do want to take my hat off once again to the French Canadian. He came of a small people. At the time of the British occupation, I doubt if there were more than a hundred thousand of them, and yet the mark they have left by their bravery and activity upon this Continent is an ineffaceable one.' He continued: 'They were more than scouts in the army. They were so far ahead that the army will take a century yet before it reaches their outposts. Brave, enduring, lighthearted, romantic, they were and are a fascinating race. The ideals of the British and of the French stock may not be the same, but while the future of the country must surely be upon British lines, the French will leave their mark deeply upon it. Five hundred years hence their blood will be looked upon as the aristocratic and distinctive blood of Canada and even as the Englishman is proud of his Norman ancestor, so the most British Canadian will proudly trace back his pedigree to the point where some ancestor had married with a Tachereau or a De Lotbiniere. It seems to me that the British cannot be too delicate in their dealings with such a people. They are not a subject people but partners in empire, and should in all ways be treated so.

'The other sight which interested us at Sault Ste. Marie was an Indian or half-breed school. The young ladies who conducted it seemed to be kindness itself, but the children struck me as mutinous little devils. Not that their actions were anything but demure and sedate, but red mutiny smouldered in their eyes. All the wrongs of their people seemed printed upon their cast-iron visages. Their race has little to complain of from the Canadian government, which has treated them with such humanity that they have really become a special endowed class living at the expense of the community . . . They are a cruel people, and in the days of torture the children were even more bloodthirsty than the rest. They are a race of caged falcons, and perhaps it is as well that they are not likely to survive the conditions which they loved.'

This thoughtless reaction and ignorance tinged with racial prejudice was most unusual for Conan Doyle. On subjects closer to his heart and his intellect, however, he was better. At a time long before John Buchan had become Governor-General of Canada, before Mordecai Richler or Margaret Atwood had been born, let alone written a word, he had this to say to the Canadian Club of Montreal about the future of the nation's literature: 'I feel, gentlemen, here in Canada that I am standing at a place which must in the process of time produce a very great literature. When I put it in the future I do not mean that it has not yet done so, but what I mean is that it will be a great volume of literature which in time to come may well influence the literature of the world. But I should be sorry to see Canada turning her whole thoughts towards such matters. It seems to me that for a strong young country with enormous practical work lying in front of it there are better things to do than dream.'

From North America he travelled back to Europe and to Britain. He could not actually see the storm clouds forming but he could feel them, sense them. For a long time he had resisted the popular feeling that war was inevitable but now he could see no other outcome of the provocation, instability and national expansion occurring in Europe. He was never a warmonger and tried in his own necessarily limited way to prevent any conflict from happening but when it happened he threw himself into it with all the passion and force that he could muster. It was some passion and some force. He wrote ceaselessly, often to the press and to the War Office and to the Prime Minister. Britain was too vulnerable, he insisted, and there were many steps that could be taken now, before it was too late. The country was not prepared for submarines and there were solutions to this threat; sailors should have life-jackets to help them if their ship was sunk; front-line soldiers needed some sort of modern body armour. All these suggestions were plausible, and most of them were taken up by the authorities and helped to save lives.

On a personal level he decided that if he was too old to serve at the front he should set up a military unit at home. He set about organizing the Civilian Reserve, investing his own money and his own time. Although there were elements of farce in this band of men otherwise unfit for military service the idea and ideal behind it were sound. Military or pseudo-military units on the domestic front reassured the populace, injected a martial spirit into civilian life and, if invasion had happened, would have been a line of defence against an army not yet as motorized and efficient as it would be a quarter of a century later. Eventually the War Office, always suspicious of anything it had not created, disbanded the Civilian Reserve but did begin a new volunteer home army. Conan Doyle immediately joined the Crowborough Company of the Sixth Royal Sussex Volunteer Regiment as an ordinary private soldier, probably the only knight in the entire force.

He thought that part-time soldiering was not enough. He had to be practical and he knew that there were more productive ways for a writer to help in the war effort. His contribution was to be a thirty-two-page pamphlet with the title *To Arms*! The Earl of Birkenhead, F.E. Smith, wrote a preface to the little sermon in favour of war and victory against the Central Powers. In this pithy example of propaganda he argued that Germany had long lusted after Britain and her empire and that the 'swaggering Junkerdom of Prussia' had to be taught a lesson. This was ironic in that Conan Doyle had only recently been fully convinced of the necessity of a war against Germany. Britain wanted nothing from this war, he said, other than justice and a peaceful and reasonable Germany. It was a noble war, a just war and clearly a conflict between good and evil.

He followed this up in 1915 by starting on his six-volume history of *The British Campaign in France and Flanders*, which would take some five years to complete. As research for this and also because he felt duty-bound to do so, in 1916 Conan Doyle visited the British, French and Italian front lines. In spite of the carnage and the devastation, he was impressed with what he found. The Boer War had accustomed him to suffering, not on such a grand scale as the Western Front but equal in its squalor. He revelled in the company of ordinary soldiers, moved to tears at their cheerful and sanguine attitude – they were there because they were there, he told friends, and were determined to make the best of it and give the Germans a good hiding. He thought the British Tommy the best sort of man in the world and blamed any defeat on incompetence from above, on bad planning or on inadequate arms. The soldiers reciprocated the feeling.

There was cheering when he toured the trenches signing autographs. The usual pattern was for a huge can of tea to be heated and poured and Conan Doyle, in his self-styled uniform of questionable military status, would sit with the men and talk, sometimes for hours. There were times when he came back to the same trench and was told that some of the men he had drunk tea and talked with were now dead. He would pause, look out at no man's land and then return to the conversation. His attitude to those who refused to fight was direct and unchanging. Pacifists and objectors were 'half-mad cranks whose absurd consciences prevented them from barring the way to the devil'. Conan Doyle was becoming more conservative with age.

This made his involvement with the case of Sir Roger Casement all the more surprising and all the more honourable. He had grown to know and respect Casement during the struggle against Belgian colonial atrocities in the Congo. Casement was an Irish nationalist who at the outbreak of the war was in New York. British rule over Ireland had to be ended, he believed, and if this meant supporting Germany then so be it. He travelled to Berlin and was used by the German government to tour POW camps and lecture Irish, and some English, soldiers about how the war was merely a fight to extend the British empire and that by fighting the British Ireland would be free, its independence guaranteed by Germany. Similar attempts were made during the Second World War by British ideologies, this time of the Nazi right, to recruit prisoners of war and then, just as in 1914 and 1915, the results were pathetic. Casement managed to convince only about fifty men to change sides and most of these had to be protected from other Irish prisoners who would have torn them apart if they could have reached them. The German military were not pleased with such a failure, particularly as its main effect was to stiffen the resolve of the other prisoners.

Added to this was the increasing public awareness of Casement's homosexuality. This was now widely known and was making several high-ranking German officers and politicians acutely uncomfortable. In 1916 he was sent by the Germans to Ireland and landed by submarine with the sole intent of aiding a resurrection against the British. Such a stab in the back was unpopular in Ireland, even when staged by fellow-Irishmen during the Easter Rising, and in Casement's case the task was hopeless. In fact almost as soon as he arrived in Ireland his mission was defeated, for a policemen challenged and then arrested him. Casement was charged with treason and in wartime this could only lead to execution if he was found guilty.

When Conan Doyle heard of this he was amazed, even incredulous. He had known Casement, liked him and certainly admired him. For Conan Doyle Casement's homosexuality was a mitigating factor rather than a further reason to despise him, as, by contrast, it was with so many members of the public and the press. Conan Doyle regarded homosexuality as 'a monstrous development' and something that was clearly 'pathological'. Casement was obviously mentally ill, he said, and it would be morally wrong to execute an insane man. So while most of the establishment and almost all popular opinion screamed for blood Conan Doyle contributed large sums of money to Casement's legal defence and campaigned for him to be treated not as a traitor but as a madman. He organized a petition against Casement's execution and persuaded his friends G.K. Chesterton, John Galsworthy and Jerome K. Jerome to sign it. He wrote letters to the press, explaining to the *Daily Chronicle* that Casement was 'a man of fine character, and that he should in the full possession of his senses act as a traitor to the country which had employed and honoured him is inconceivable to anyone who knew him. He had, it is true, a strong prepossession in favour of Germany before the war, but this was due to his belief that she was destined to challenge the Monroe Doctrine, which Casement bitterly resented as being the ultimate cause of all that Putumayo barbarism which he had officially to investigate. [As consul-general in Rio de Janeiro before the war he had denounced atrocities in the rubber industry.] I may say that I disagreed with him upon the subject, but in all our discussion I have never heard him say a word which was disloyal to Great Britain. He was a sick man, however, worn by tropical hardships, and he complained often of pains in his head. Last May I had letters from him from Ireland which seemed to me so wild that I expressed fears at the time as to the state of his nerves. I have no doubt that he is not in a normal state of mind, and that this unhappy escapade at Berlin is only an evidence of it. On the face of it, would any sane man expect an assurance about Ireland which had obviously been already broken about Belgium?'

It was to no avail. Sir Roger was executed and the people cheered. Arthur Conan Doyle did not.

On 6 February 1914 Conan Doyle had written in answer to a question: 'The *Strand* are paying so high a price for this story that I should be churlish indeed if I refused any possible information.

'The name, I think, will be 'The Valley of Fear'. Speaking from the present possibilities it should run to not less than 50,000 words. I have done nearly 25,000, I reckon roughly. With luck I should finish it before the end of March.

'As in the 'Study in Scarlet' the plot goes to America for at least half the book while it recounts the events which led up to the crime in England which has engaged Holmes' services . . . But of course in this long stretch we abandon Holmes. That is necessary.'

The book turned out to be one of Conan Doyle's greatest creations. Actually 'The Valley of Fear' is two stories, each of which can be read almost without reference to the other. The first, 'The Tragedy of Birlstone', tells of a country-house murder in Sussex with the involvement of Professor Moriarty. The second, 'The Scowrers', is more elaborate. Set in the 1870s, it depicts the industrial, social and political conflict in America between Irish miners and their English–American employers and the development of a secret brotherhood of Irish agitators. This group was modelled strongly on the Molly Maguires. The stories were serialized in the *Strand* between September 1914 and May 1915 and in spite of the real horror taking place across the Channel and even in the streets of London they did extremely well.

His Last Bow, the penultimate collection of Holmes tales, followed soon afterwards and featured only eight stories, the shortest Holmes collection that Conan Doyle wrote. It was probably supposed to represent the last appearance of Sherlock Holmes but in now time-honoured fashion this would not be the case. The stories are: 'The Adventure of Wisteria Lodge', 'The Adventure of the Red Circle', 'The Adventure of the Bruce-Partington Plans', 'The Adventure of the Dying Detective', 'The Disappearance of Lady Frances Carfax', 'The Adventure of the Devil's Foot', the eponymous 'His Last Bow' and 'The Cardboard Box'. This last story had originally appeared in *The Memoirs of Sherlock Holmes* but was removed from all editions after 1894 and included in *His Last Bow*. Four of them are especially noteworthy. 'Wisteria Lodge' is a long story, originally published in magazine form in two parts. Conan Doyle uses his knowledge of voodoo to bring to life a somewhat complicated and shocking story. 'I find it recorded in my notebook that it was a bleak and windy day towards the end of March in the year 1895. Holmes had received a telegram whilst we sat at our lunch, and he had scribbled a reply. He made no remark, but the matter remained in his thoughts, for he stood in front of the fire afterwards with a thoughtful face, smoking his pipe, and casting an occasional glance at the message. Suddenly he turned upon me with a mischievous twinkle in his eyes.

'"I suppose, Watson, we must look upon you as a man of letters," said he. "How do you define the word grotesque?"'

'The Adventure of the Bruce-Partington Plans' sees the return of Holmes's brother Mycroft, last seen in 'The Greek Interpreter'. This story struck a chord during the war owing to its discussion of treason, espionage and the secret plans for a submarine. A decent, loyal English patriot is murdered and his courageous fiancée refuses to believe that he has betrayed his country and instead demands justice. 'The Adventure of the Dying Detective' enabled Conan Doyle to use his medical knowledge to the full. Here Holmes pretends to be dying of a terrible illness but it is a clever device to catch an enemy.

'His Last Bow' differs from all the other Holmes stories in that it is narrated in the third person and not by Dr Watson. Holmes comes out of retirement in Sussex to work on a case of espionage just before the outbreak of the war. Conan Doyle uses the piece as a vehicle to attack the Germans, Irish extremists and the suffragettes. The story, and the collection, ends with: 'Good old Watson! You are the one fixed point in a changing age. There's an east wind coming all the same, such a wind as never blew on England yet. It will be cold and bitter, Watson, and a good many of us may wither before its blast. But it's God's own wind none the less, and a cleaner, better, stronger land will lie in the sunshine when the storm has cleared.'

Cold and bitter it most certainly was. As the war neared its end and as the toll of bodies mounted, Conan Doyle spent ever more time reading, writing and thinking about spiritualism. Yet the wind still blew. And it blew on Kingsley Doyle. In October, 1917 Conan Doyle was lecturing in Nottingham. He received a telegram from his daughter Mary explaining that his son was dying of influenza and pneumonia after having been wounded on the Somme. Conan Doyle cried, just a little, and then went out to deliver his lecture, on the subject of spiritualism. He learnt of Kingsley's death shortly afterwards, on Armistice Day. The wind kept blowing.

7

Not Faith but Knowledge

Conan Doyle published his first full book on the subject of spiritualism, *The New Revelation*, just as the war was ending. There had never been, he said, such an appropriate time for such a volume. Entire towns had disappeared, communities had been expunged from the face of the earth, every family had lost a loved one and grieving mothers, widows, sisters, brothers and fathers seemed to be everywhere. On a personal level Conan Doyle was also deeply affected. Apart from the death of so many friends and acquaintances there had been the death of his son and in February 1919 the death of his younger brother, Innes, whom he had looked after and cared for. Innes, a brigadier general, was also struck by pneumonia and soon died. Two years after the end of the war, in 1920, the ultimate blow came. Conan Doyle's mother, Mary, died. It was not a surprise as she was in her eighties and had been ill for a while but even so the loss hit Conan Doyle in a way he could not have predicted.

Mary Doyle had led a full and usually happy life and had known the love and respect of her family, and certainly of Arthur, but this did not ease his pain. He had confided in her, used her as sage and adviser, told her things he did not even tell his wife. Her counsel was invariably correct and incisive and suddenly it was no longer there. Kingsley and Innes were mere youths and had had the bulk of their lives taken away from them. Mary had led most of hers, but even so he could not stop thinking and worrying about what life would be like without 'the Ma'am', always there to listen and to respond. A mother fixation? Perhaps, but not of any sinister kind. Better to call it a close relationship that occasionally, but seldom, became too exclusive.

The deaths, the letters from grieving people asking for advice or an explanation, all contributed to this latest explosion of spiritualism in Conan Doyle. He was not alone. This was the era of the spiritualist, the epoch of the seance. The final chapter of Conan Doyle's autobiography is entitled 'The Psychic Quest', and from 1918 until his death twelve years later spiritualism eclipsed every other subject. He had, of course, been interested in the subject since he was a young man but all that seemed like mere play when compared with the seriousness of the postwar situation.

'I have not obtruded the psychic question upon the reader, though it has grown in importance with the years, and has now come to absorb the whole energy of my life,' he wrote in his memoirs. 'I cannot, however, close these scattered memories of my adventures in thought and action without some reference, however incomplete, to that which has been far the most important thing in my life. It is the thing for which every preceding phase, my gradual religious development, my books, my modest fortune, which enables me to devote myself to less lucrative work, my platform work, which helps me to convey the message, and my physical strength, which is still sufficient to stand arduous tours and to fill the largest halls for an hour and a half with my voice, have each and all been an unconscious preparation. For thirty years I have trained myself exactly for the role without the least inward suspicion of whither I was tending.'

The New Revelation was a public declaration, an open shout that Conan Doyle was a spiritualist. Any teenage gesture, any support for the theory and faith when he was a younger man, was irrelevant compared with now. This was the creator of Sherlock Holmes and Professor Challenger, the hero of the Boer War and the champion of the ordinary soldier and of the empire, insisting that he believed in spiritualism. By the beginning of the third chapter, 'The Coming Life', he had outlined the modifications that would have to take place in contemporary Christianity and then took on the eternal question of what occurs to people after death. 'The evidence on this point is fairly full and consistent. Messages from the dead have been received in many lands at various times, mixed up with a good deal about the world, which we could verify. When messages come thus, it is only fair, I think, to suppose that if what we can test is true then what we cannot test is also true. When in addition we find a very great uniformity in the messages and an agreement as to details which are not at all in accordance with any pre-existing scheme of thought, then I think the presumption of truth is very strong. It is difficult to think that some fifteen or twenty messages from various sources of which I have personal notes, all agree, and yet are all wrong, nor is it easy to suppose that spirits can tell the truth about our world but untruth about their own.

'I received lately, in the same week, two accounts of life in the next world, one received through the hand of the near relative of a high dignitary of the Church, while the other came through the wife of a working mechanician in Scotland. Neither could have been aware of the existence of the other, and yet the two accounts are so like as to be practically the same.

'The message upon these points seems to me to be infinitely reassuring, whether we regard our own fate or that' of our friends. The departed all agree that passing is usually both easy and painless, and followed by an enormous reaction of peace and ease. The individual finds himself in a spirit body, which is the exact counterpart of his old one, save that all disease, weakness, or deformity has passed from it. This body is standing or floating beside the old body, and conscious both of it and of the surrounding people. At this moment the dead man is nearer to matter than he will ever be again, and hence it is that at that moment the greater part of those cases occur where, his thoughts having turned to someone in the distance, the spirit body went with the thoughts and was manifest to the person.'

'Reassuring' – the key word. The other chapters of the book have titles such as 'The Search', 'The Next Phase of Life' and 'Automatic Writing', making it a miniature Bible of spiritualism, a single-volume handbook and guide to the world beyond and the passage to it. Conan Doyle chose two particular examples of the many cases that had convinced him of the validity of spiritualism, people who had communicated from their life and death. The first centred on a young Australian woman named Dorothy Post-lethwaite, who had died in Melbourne at the age of sixteen. She explained that those who had departed their earthly bodies lived in a sphere that circled the earth, where there was no physical but some mental pain and where everybody was taken care of and, ominously, chastised if they broke the moral code. There were no barriers of race, religion or philosophy and everybody eventually arrived in the sphere, whether they wanted to or not. She also communicated the fact that a superior race of highly intelligent beings lived on Mars. The other talkative spirit was a cricketer whom Conan Doyle had known and who told him after death that families existed in the spirit world but that earthly marriage was considered no reason to reunite couples. People who were genuinely in love, however, did meet up.

Conan Doyle and Jean had been invited to a seance in Wales in early 1919. In the nineteenth and early twentieth century Wales had been home to a series of revivals, enthusiasms and mass conversions, ranging from Methodism to Socialism, and now spiritualism. In a mining village in the south called Penylan lived two brothers, Tom and Will Thomas. Their father had been a committed spiritualist for more than forty years and had founded and become president of the Merthyr Spiritualist Society, and their mother and sisters were all active mediums. The whole family were known throughout Wales and, in a spiritualist context, throughout the world. Their spirit guide, as was so often the case, was a native Indian, by the name of White Eagle. Because of their influence and fame Tom and Will Thomas managed to attract celebrities and influential people, among them Sir Arthur Conan Doyle.

This particular seance was held in the home of another well-known spiritualist, a Mr Wall, and among the guests were a local MP called Lee Joseph, the Chief Constable of Cardiff and more than a dozen leading spiritualists. Everyone present participated in a thorough investigation of the room and the rest of the house to find out if there were any hidden doors or secret entrances. Nothing was found. Cardiff's leading policemen tied Tom up with a thick rope to a heavy chair, the audience and the participants sung hymns in Welsh and English and then the lights were turned off. Within a few seconds objects began to fly around the room in unpredictable directions. A tambourine stunned everyone when it noisily hit the ceiling, bounced off a wall and then landed on the floor. More shocking was the flight of a doll, which looked almost human as it whirled around the room, passing close to the heads of the onlookers.

All this time Tom had apparently been in a trance, saying nothing. Suddenly he broke his silence and addressed a question to Jean. He asked her if she felt cold. She said that she did. Without warning a heavy jacket that belonged to Will fell into her lap. As Jean tentatively put on the jacket more objects, including a guitar and a trumpet, flew around the place. The combined effect of the singing of hymns, the crashing of metal and wood, the shrieks of fear and surprise and the occasional humming of the Thomas brothers was overwhelming. When the session eventually came to an end the Chief Constable and his assistant took a close look at the bound medium and found that in their opinion the ropes around him had not been touched and he was still in the same place and position as when they had originally tied him up.

'I believe that we are dealing with a thoroughly material generation,' Conan Doyle wrote of this gathering in his introduction to Sydney A. Mosley's *An Amazing Seance and an Exposure*, 'with limited and self-satisfied religious and scientific lines of thought, which can only be broken up and finally rearranged by the shock of encountering physical phenomena which are outside their philosophies. The whole campaign is, I believe, engineered from the other side, and one can continually catch glimpses of wisdom and purpose beyond that of the world. The levitation of the tambourine or the moving of furniture may seem humble and even ludicrous phenomena, but the more thoughtful mind understands that the nature of the object is immaterial, and that the real question has to do with the force that moves it.'

In a correspondence with H.G. Wells at the time of this seance Conan Doyle told his cynical acquaintance that while people like Wells, of the 'enlightened' left, progressive and often atheistic, despised prejudice as being archaic, anti-modern and small-minded, they evinced nothing but prejudice on the subject of spiritualism and the issues surrounding it. If someone described France as a country in which most of the people spoke German, he said, without ever having been to France, spoken to a French person or having read any books about the country, we would dismiss him as being either arrogant or stupid. Yet people mock and condemn spiritualism without having been to a seance, without having read any sophisticated books on the subject and before they have spoken to intelligent and reasonable people who believed in it.[1]

For every respected medium, however, there was the antithesis in the form of a campaigner or journalist bent on exposing spiritualism as a sham. Some of these people had a genuine regard for what they thought of as being the truth, some had been damaged and hurt by fake mediums who had pretended to make contact with a deceased relative but were simply performing conjuring tricks and others were no more than writers in search of a juicy story concerning famous but apparently foolish people. The motives of the editor of the *Sunday Express*, James Douglas, are not known but he had certainly made a career out of exposing fraudulent mediums. As soon as the Welsh seance with Conan Doyle became well known Douglas offered a prize of £500 to any spiritualist, guide or medium who could prove beyond all doubt that he or she had made contact with someone who had recently died. It was a measure of Conan Doyle's fame in the years following the war that anything he was involved with became a matter of interest to press and public alike. Douglas knew a story when he saw one. He dearly wanted to draw Conan Doyle into his coverage and, if possible, have him write a defence of spiritualism for the *Sunday Express*.

If the munificent sum of £500 was to be paid, Douglas insisted that a specialized jury be assembled, consisting of himself and a group of professional magicians, clergymen and scientists who had experience of seances and mediums. Tom and Will Thomas were less than enthusiastic about the proposal, having been humiliated in public before by clever, capable and profoundly sceptical people. The spirits could not be commanded, their work could not be demanded, they said, and Conan Doyle supported them in their reservations. Moreover, if the spirits and the denizens of the world beyond knew that they were being judged for mere sport and gain they might well play silly tricks and abandon their mediums all together.

But public pressure was mounting now. It was to be a repeated problem for Conan Doyle and his spiritualist friends that whenever a challenge was brought the public became so enthusiastic that to decline the test would have looked like an admission of defeat and failure. He spoke to Douglas directly and insisted that a certain decorum and respect be granted to the proceedings, as it would be to any religious gathering. He also joined the Thomas brothers in demanding that one particular magician and notorious opponent of spiritualism be barred from the jury, but added that he would not take part in such a farce. Conditions discussed and accepted by both sides, the supervised seance took place in the offices of the *Sunday Express*. The two brothers were tied to strong chairs with thick ropes and then, as was usual in these events, people tended to see what they wanted to see. The spiritualists in the audience swore to a presence in the room and to a small white, efflorescent cloud that had formed in the corner. The most significant occurrence was that one spiritualist claimed that a pair of trouser braces had landed in his lap. Not a bit of it, said the critics. There was no cloud and nobody else actually saw the braces move and materialize.

In the absence of a clear outcome no money was paid, though the circulation of the *Sunday Express* increased steadily, and the paper decided to stage another test. This time the person who came forward was an experienced professional magician and conjurer. He had exposed and also worked with numerous false mediums over the years but had undergone a conversion and believed that spiritualism was a valid belief. He knew of a medium in London and the seance would take place in her flat, though with a specialized audience of seven people. The medium proceeded to give details of people's clothing that they had left at their homes or had once worn. She was then tightly and firmly bound, the lights were turned down and the onlookers held their breath in anticipation. Something seemed to happen. A white vapour, similar to that which had been produced at the previous *Sunday Express* seance, appeared to materialize from the medium. This was followed by a bright, almost stunning ray of light. Was this proof? Apparently not enough; the £500 was going to be extremely difficult to collect.

After this event Conan Doyle realized that he had to become involved in these test seances, no matter how vulgar and awkward they might be. He was simply missing the boat. He joined a select committee of people, including Sir Henry Lunn, Lady Glenconner, a superintendent from the Metropolitan Police and the editors of the *Occult Review* and of *Light*, for which Conan Doyle had been writing some articles and reviews. They examined this same medium who had produced the light and the vapour and challenged her to read certain words and articles locked in a special box. She appeared to be able to do this. Next came the medium's depiction of a black swan, which referred to a Swan pen carried by Sir Henry Lunn. The event that followed this was extremely emotional and a little disturbing to Conan Doyle. The medium spoke of a ring belonging to Kingsley. When the lights were turned on the medium was still tied up and there were no signs of tampering.

Conan Doyle told the *Sunday Express*: 'She was able to tell me the initials on the ring of my boy – who died some months ago – although the average person examining it would perhaps make nothing of it. It was so worn that it would be excusable if you could not make anything of it even if you had the ring before you. So far as the second part of the programme was concerned, that is a different matter. Before a decision can be made, one must attend several seances with the same medium. One certainly saw a floating light. But although I was sitting in the front row, and was quite close to it, I could not make anything of it. I should have to see it again before passing a definite opinion on it. In any case, I think that the proceedings were instructive and clear. But I have my doubts about the whole thing.' He was right to be sceptical. The identification of the letters on the ring could be easily explained – Conan Doyle was a world-famous man and anyone who had followed his career would be aware of the son and brother he had lost during the war and also of the ring that he prized so dearly. As for the other phenomena, none of them was beyond rational explanation if those present were prepared to accept a degree of dishonesty and trickery on the part of the medium and her friends, but Sir Henry Lunn and Lady Glenconner in particular would have none of this. And how Conan Doyle himself wanted to believe in it all. Yet although he was credulous he was not naive and that was to the good, for his reputation as well as his peace of mind. Only days after the investigated seance those involved admitted that it had all been an elaborate hoax.

The *Sunday Express* was now no longer the only newspaper covering the story of Conan Doyle and the spiritualists – the subject was the talk of Fleet Street. He managed to bring Sherlock Holmes back from the dead, they joked, so why not have conversations with dead people the world over? Because of the press coverage he received letters from mediums, magicians and assorted spiritualists from all over Europe and as far afield as Canada and New Zealand. Most of them he ignored, some he replied to politely but without investigation, and a special few he pursued. One was from a London medium who specialized in tracing sons lost in war for their grieving mothers. He decided to establish a newspaper committee representing the *Sunday Express*, *Daily Chronicle*, *Evening Standard*, *Daily Sketch* and *Daily Mail* and together they set about investigating the claims of the medium. The results were encouraging and accurate, and then seemed to be confirmed when she worked with Conan Doyle and repeatedly referred to his son as 'Kingsley'. This was actually his middle name – his first name, Alleyne, was used only by his immediate family. Yet once again Conan Doyle was underestimating the public's knowledge of his private and personal life. The medium then managed to make contact with Innes, who satisfied his brother that he was the genuine article. Conan Doyle was convinced but the journalists on the panel did not agree with him. The £500 was never paid to anyone. Journalists from rival newspapers enjoyed explaining that they were not at all surprised.

In October 1919 Conan Doyle was asked by the Bishop of Worcester to deliver a lecture on spiritualism in the city's cathedral. The very invitation from the episcopal lord provoked a stream of letters to the Anglican press from people who associated spiritualism with satanic worship and anti-Christianity. Yet the lecture went well. Enemies of spiritualism in the Church of England demanded a right of reply, however, and an orthodox Christian and conservative cleric named Canon James Wilson was invited to respond. Before very long the local newspaper, the *Worcestershire Advertiser*, fuelled the debate and asked both men to write articles further explaining their position. The story was by now being covered well beyond the confines of Worcestershire.

Canon Wilson delivered another lecture in which he gave a short speech on the history of Christianity and then explained that most spiritualism consisted of either bunk or ignorance, while whatever limited supernatural force might exist was both minimal and, more importantly, potentially dangerous and hostile to God. Letters continued in the press, rival lectures were delivered and seconds came to support their champions Conan Doyle and Wilson. As with most of the arguments Conan Doyle had over the years about spiritualism, nobody was proved correct and nobody was willing to admit defeat. What is notable is the lengths to which a nationally respected clergyman went to defend his faith against spiritualism. We can construe from this that spiritualism was not the meagre movement that so many of its enemies tried to paint it as and was in fact in direct competition, in numbers as well as influence, with the established churches.

If Worcestershire was not wholly convinced, there was always a welcome in the valleys and hillsides of Wales. This time another Welsh medium, Evan Powell, met Conan Doyle on the lecture circuit and impressed him with his obvious disregard for payment or praise. He seemed to care only for the meaning and the results of spiritualism. One evening the two men retired to Conan Doyle's hotel room with Jean and their friends and fellow-spiritualist activists Frank Blake and Henry Engholm. Powell was frisked in standard fashion for hidden pockets or concealed devices and then tied to his chair. He was given a specially painted megaphone that would be constantly visible in the dark and then the lights were turned off. Within moments a spirit named Black Hawk spoke through Powell and made the megaphone whirl around the room. Then Black Hawk announced, 'Leely wishes to speak with the Lady of the Wigwam.' Jean was convinced that this was her deceased friend Lily Loder-Symonds. Other objects were then moved around the room and nobody could work out how. The seance was taking place in a hotel room which only a skilled burglar could have entered without notice. More significant, it had been Conan Doyle's idea to choose that particular venue, so it was impossible that anything or anyone could have been planted or hidden there before the seance. They met again the next day, and Conan Doyle's life was changed for ever.

'Then came what to me was the supreme moment of my spiritual experience. It is almost too sacred for full description, and yet I feel that God sends such gifts that we may share them with others. Then came a voice in the darkness, a whispered voice, saying "Jean, it is I". I heard the word "Father". I said "Dear boy is that you?" I had then a sense of a face very near my own, and of breathing. Then the clear voice came again with an intensity and note very distinctive of my son, "Forgive me!" I told him eagerly that I had no grievance of any kind. A large, strong hand then rested upon my head, it was gently bent forward, and I felt and heard a kiss just above my brow. "Tell me, dear, are you happy?" I cried. There was silence, and I feared he was gone. Then on a sighing note came the words, "Yes I am so happy." A moment afterwards another gentle voice, claiming to be that of my wife's mother, recently deceased, was heard in front of us. We could not have recognised the voice as we could the other. A few loving words were said, and then a small warm hand patted both our cheeks with a little gesture which was full of affection. Such were my experiences.'[2]

In 1919 Conan Doyle completed and published *The Vital Message*, the second of his spiritualist works, and to publicize and promote the book he went on a long lecture tour and book-signing trip. These progresses through the land were exhausting and almost certainly, in the longer term, hastened the writer's death. One of the reasons was that he was a deeply conscientious performer, writing new speeches for almost every venue and thoroughly rehearsing them. The drain on his energy was colossal, the material reward very limited. The tour following the publication of *The Vital Message* took him all over the country – to an audience of 2000 in Birmingham and to similarly sized gatherings in Huddersfield, Manchester, Portsmouth, Glasgow and Nottingham. During the tour he told one journalist that spiritualism had to be understood in context and had to be appreciated for its potential and future.

'Men have largely ceased to go to church. It is not that they are irreligious. It is that they have outgrown this presentiment of religion. Is it not remarkable that in the lectures that I have delivered up and down the country quite half my audience are men?' He continued by saying that spiritualism 'is a religion that approaches that of the early Christian church. Christ was the great Psychic, and his disciples, I believe, were chosen because they were his psychics.' He concluded: 'It is essential, therefore, to hold the sittings in a reverent and religious atmosphere. Thus may they be "the communion of saints". We begin with prayers and hymns. It is either the most solemn thing in the world or it is absolute nonsense. There is no middle ground between these extremes.'[3]

From England Conan Doyle crossed the sea to Northern Ireland to see Dr W.J. Crawford at Queen's University, Belfast. Crawford taught Mechanical Engineering and throughout the war had been exploring spiritualism from a scientific basis. He had discovered a local family, the Gollghers, who claimed great spiritualistic powers, particularly the youngest member, Kathleen. Crawford tested Kathleen and the rest of her family in their own home but did everything he could to guarantee fairness and openness in these seances. It is interesting that in such experiments even the most sincere of spiritualists tended to leave themselves open to some form of criticism and disbelief – an open window, an unobserved intruder or an audience composed of friends and sympathizers. The same happened here, with Crawford genuinely not realizing – or not appreciating the damage that could be done to his tests by any solidly based criticism – that most of the people observing the Gollgher seances were eager for them to be convincing.

Yet he knew most of the tricks that could be played by the frauds in the spiritualist business. He wrote about his experiments in 1920 in *The Psychic Structures at the Gollgher Circle*, which was published after his death, Crawford having taken his own life. Before this tragedy he had formed a distinct spiritualist theory based on the existence of 'psychic rods'. These phenomena extended from the medium and could lift and project any object or even people. Crawford claimed to have felt, even held these rods and could not explain them. He tried everything he knew to trace them, to uncover some mechanical or fraudulent origin, but try as he might he could not succeed. Furthermore, he also found the rods were accompanied by a thick film or slime that he referred to as 'plasma'. This substance appeared to emanate from the medium's feet, so Crawford tried to cover Kathleen Gollgher's feet in an effort to explain the plasma. In an absurd but thorough operation he also asked the girl to change her stockings and knickers before each test – the poor young woman went through dozens of sets of underwear. With the help of a female nurse Crawford gave the girl an intimate examination and concluded that the plasma came from between her legs. He photographed the girl, published some of the pictures and, for reasons of decorum and discretion, held others back.

Conan Doyle was fascinated by this development. These new discoveries confirmed the sophistication of spiritualism. This was not magic, but was a form of science mingled with theology. 'Among the experimenters we have a material school who urge that we are finding some extraordinary latent property of the normal body, and we have another school, to which the author belongs, who believe that we have come upon a link which may be part of a chain leading to some new order of life. It should be added that there is nothing concerning it which has not been known to the old alchemists of the Middle Ages.' He went on to write: 'Personally the author is of the opinion that several different forms of plasma with different activities will be discovered, the whole forming a separate science of the future which may well be called Plasmology.'[4]

This interest in the origins of plasma intrigued Conan Doyle. He made contact with Dr Gustave Geley of France's Institut Métaphysique, who eventually became a close family friend. Geley had been experimenting with spiritualism and spiritualists for some years and under laboratory conditions had conducted a series of tests with two well-known mediums, Madame Bisson and Eva C. During one of these the naked Eva C. had all her orifices closely examined before being dressed in a skin-tight uniform that was sewn up so that nothing could get in or out. Unusually the lights were not turned down or off for these experiments and everything could be clearly seen. Plasma regularly appeared, often seeming to cause pain to the medium, who would groan, sometimes scream, as the substance materialized. The plasma came from her fingers, nipples and vagina and even from inside her mouth. This 'ectoplasm' could move around, expand and reduce and disappear completely at will. It could also take on different shapes, sometimes taking on the form of a human face or limb. It was just as he had expected, said Conan Doyle, and it all served to confirm his beliefs that twentieth-century spiritualists had merely scratched the surface of this wonderful revelation.

For the last ten years of his life Conan Doyle effectively became the missionary-in-chief of world spiritualism. As such he was the main target of spiritualism's opponents. Enemies accused him of monomania and said that he should never have been distracted from writing fiction, or that he had never in fact moved away from writing fiction. In January 1920 Joseph McCabe spoke to a large crowd in the Patrick Burgh Hall in Glasgow on what he offensively entitled 'Sir A. Conan Doyle's Ghosts'. He thundered from the platform that Conan Doyle might not be a bad one but he was still a foolish one. By giving his influential backing to spiritualism, to table moving, to ghosts and to conversations with the dead, he was hurting the parents of those brave young men who had died in the war. Let us remember their memories, recall them as they really were, he exhorted, and not pretend that they are still here or hidden just around a corner, able to be resurrected vicariously by a medium who, oddly enough, usually required a payment for their altruistic services. He would very much like, he said, to take on the great Sir Arthur Conan Doyle personally. Conan Doyle heard of these comments the following morning and, never one to refuse a challenge, wondered if Joseph McCabe would be willing to keep to his word and meet his nemesis in verbal combat. It is likely that Conan Doyle thought that McCabe was making an empty bluff. He wasn't.

The two men met on 11 March at the Queen's Hall in London. When the debate was announced all the official tickets were soon taken. As the evening approached fake tickets were sold on the black market and valid ones changed hands for inflated prices. People travelled from as far afield as Aberdeen, the Isle of Wight and even the European mainland. One member of the crowd, an enthusiastic supporter of Conan Doyle, had come all the way from Stockholm. The writer believed that it was his duty to defend spiritualism wherever and whenever it was challenged and that he was the best person to do the job. It was now a vocation. For his part Joseph McCabe, along with the Rationalist Press Association, believed that this was the good fight that had to be won. Facing each other were two very able, two very determined, men. The scene was set for one of the most impressive debates of the era.

McCabe began by ripping in to the spiritualist fathers, those men who had done so much to establish the modern spiritualism that he so despised. D.D. Howe, for example, a long-time influence on Conan Doyle, was a charlatan, said McCabe. He lived all his life off spiritualism and its gullible adherents, married only to secure more wealth and even inherited more than £36,000 from one feeble-minded woman, a Mrs Lyon, by telling her that her beloved husband, now in the world beyond, had demanded that his and his wife's money be left to none other than D.D. Howe. As for Conan Doyle himself, McCabe said, 'I submit to this jury that, like every man who has gone into that dim supernatural world, he has lived in clouds, in a mist. Whatever other witnesses there may be, you will find that distortion of judgement, that blearing of vision, which occurs whenever a man enters that wonderful world, that world of almost unparalleled trickery in the history of man.'

Conan Doyle had been known to lose his temper and his friends and family prayed that he would not do so this time. Such a response would be fatal and McCabe wanted nothing so much as an aggressive reaction. Conan Doyle had been in this position before. He sipped from the glass of water in front of him on the podium, smiled, took a deep breath and paused as he looked at the audience. He began slowly, almost laughing as he dealt with his opponent. If only McCabe had studied the subject properly, he said, he would know so much more and would be able to approach it intelligently and in an enlightened manner.

The writer then performed a dramatic gesture that he

had been preparing for ever since the debate had been announced. He took from his jacket pocket a small, black leather-covered notebook. In this book, he said, I have the names of 160 people – politicians, diplomats, authors, scientists, generals, admirals, businessmen and artists – who believed without any doubt or question in the truth of spiritualism. Were these men fools and dunderheads? When these grand sailors led ships into deadly battle against Germany's navy were they idiotic and impractical? When these cabinet ministers decided on affairs of state that could affect the world were they uneducated or callow? The questions were rhetorical and the audience was swaying towards this elegant Scottish gentleman who refused to be provoked. 'They have not been to one seance, like Mr Clodd, or to two or three, like Mr McCabe. Many have studied for twenty or thirty years, and have been to hundreds of seances. When it comes to people who have never had any practical experience, simply because they think and reason so, arguing against men who have taken the trouble and done the work, then I say they are out of court.' There was a spontaneous round of applause and some in the audience even stood up to show their approval.

He then went on to defend D.D. Howe. It was easy to attack a man's character when he could not defend himself, he said, and also cowardly and dishonourable. Howe did not ask for any money and seldom got any – it was too facile and certainly inaccurate to throw the motive of financial gain at various spiritualists. Were not clergymen paid, did not the Archbishop of Canterbury receive any compensation on earth? There was more laughter, and now some cheering. As to the nasty allegations about a sum of money being left to him by a friend, McCabe had that all wrong as well. First, the sum was not £36,000 but £24,000 and if McCabe had got that basic fact wrong, what else might he have mistaken? Second, the money was given without coercion and after the fact the unstable Mrs Lyon demanded the money back and took the case to court, where Howe was completely exonerated.

From this point Conan Doyle felt that the audience was with him. He told little jokes, and digressed just enough to win the confidence of the doubters. He was doing well, perhaps giving the best address of his career. He discussed plasma and ectoplasm. He spoke of the experiences of Madame Bisson, of Dr Geley, of Eva C., and of the writings and work of a German investigator, Dr Schrenck-Notzing. Here McCabe rushed to respond. He claimed that Eva C. was one of those rare creatures, a 'ruminant' who could swallow large objects and then regurgitate them from her stomach and out of her mouth. As for the others mentioned, they were all working together, all friends and allies aiming for a common goal. The crowd began to boo at this. 'That's no argument,' shouted one member of the audience and was promptly told to be quiet and not interrupt. Conan Doyle took this chance to interject. There are thousands of different photographs of all this, he said, and even if McCabe could dismiss some of them he surely could not explain every one. McCabe frowned but said nothing.

Conan Doyle continued, explaining that the young Dr Schrenck-Notzing, a man of spotless reputation and the finest scholarship, had made all his tests of the mediums he met progressively more rigorous. What was so interesting, he said, was that investigators from all over the world found that when they explored the origin of plasma and ectoplasm they all found that it came from the vaginal area and from between a woman's legs. At this several members of the audience coughed a little louder than was strictly necessary. He paused and then continued. Had McCabe properly studied the writings of Schrenk-Notzing? He had written: 'Assuming that a female medium wished to use the vagina as a hiding-place for closely rolled packets, e.g. chiffon gauze, she would have to attach some kind of cord or ribbon to the packet beforehand in order to be able to withdraw it. This cord would be detected during the exploration at the mouth of the vagina, and my finger introduced into the vagina would feel the foreign body. In the case of persons with a very wide vaginal entrance, it might be possible to withdraw the packets by means of the fingers deeply inserted. But such a manipulation supposes that the genitals are not separated from the hand by any partition, even a knitted one, and that the person is in a standing or reclining position. She might have touched the external genitals through the garment, but could not have penetrated to any depth.

'The hiding of objects in the anal aperture, and their withdrawal from it, is even less possible, on account of its closure by a firm ring muscle, which hinders the introduction of a finger. Hidden packets can only be withdrawn by means of a cord of suitable length. The external end of which would have been immediately discovered during the corporeal examination; but never with the sole help of the person's own finger.'

Pretty strong stuff in 1920. And there was more. Yes, Conan Doyle said, there were people who were born with or trained themselves to develop, the ability to vomit up objects previously in their stomach, some of a very large size. But any doctor would know, and common sense should tell us, that when this occurred the object was not pristine but would be covered with foods, stomach acids and slime. It would also smell distinctly of the stomach, detectable to anybody who knew anything of the subject.

Gradually the debate wound down, becoming stuck on technicalities and points of information that could not be directly contradicted but did not in any way enlighten the audience. At the end of the evening both men received a standing ovation but, as reporters from the newspaper and members of the audience noticed, the one for Conan Doyle was longer and louder, and included cheers and whistles.

By this time he was able to combine his desire to spread the word of empire with his divine obsession with spiritualism, which had become the twin lecturing subjects of the last decade of his life. He had been invited to travel across Australia giving talks and being interviewed. Would he come? He would like to, but he was no longer prepared to travel without his wife and three children. The cost of the trip would be colossal but agents both in Britain and Australia were sure a large profit could still be made. In the middle of August 1920 the Conan Doyles sailed off, arriving in Australia almost five weeks later. The lecture tour began in Adelaide, where a largely spiritualist audience were delighted with what they heard. He travelled on to Melbourne and adored the city, thinking that it resembled the better parts of the Edinburgh of his youth. In Melbourne he met Charles Bailey, who had an international reputation as a medium and scholar with an expertise in the mysterious appearance of previously unseen objects at seances. Conan Doyle knew that this man had probably indulged in fraud in the past – he had produced two birds and their nests seemingly out of nowhere, until a local pet-shop owner had identified him as the man who earlier the same day had purchased a pair of birds – but friends of Conan Doyle assured him that these were rash acts committed under pressure and that Bailey was in reality a gifted medium. A seance was arranged and the writer sat through the entire session. The results were not quite as he expected but he was still convinced of the media's authenticity.

'The results were far above all possible fraud, both in the conditions and in the articles brought into the room by the spirit power. For example, I have a detailed account published by Dr D.W. McCarthy of Sydney, under the title, "Rigid Tests of the Occult". During these tests Bailey was sealed up in a bag, and in one case was inside a cage of mosquito curtain. The door and windows were sealed and the fireplace blocked. The sitters were all personal friends, but they mutually searched each other. The medium was stripped naked before the seance. Under these stringent conditions during a series of six sittings 130 articles were brought into the room, which included eighty-seven ancient coins (mostly of Ptolemy), eight live birds, eighteen precious stones of modest value and varied character, two live turtles, seven inscribed Babylonian tablets, one Egyptian scarabaus, an Arabic newspaper, a leopard skin, four nests and many other things. I may add that at a previous test meeting they have had a young live shark about one and one half feet long, which was tangled with wet sea-weed and flopped about on the table.'

From Melbourne the family moved to Sydney. At a reception for 3500 people Conan Doyle spoke about the need for thorough and professional psychic investigation. He was publicly criticized by the local president of the Christian Evidence Society, who challenged him to a public debate. Conan Doyle refused on the grounds that there simply was not the time and that he was just too tired. The response was taken badly and used against Conan Doyle – the man is scared of argument, the critics said; he can't stand up to the tougher arguments of the Australian anti-spiritualists. They treat him too softly and kindly in Britain, they said, and it's rather different here. Actually it wasn't and Conan Doyle would probably not have taken very long to dispose of the arguments of his Sydney opponents. The fact was that he was learning, at last, to use his time with more care and selection. He was feeling his age.

While he was in Australia Conan Doyle wrote to the spiritualist Sir Oliver Lodge in Britain and told him about a series of photographs that he had been sent of so-called fairies. He wanted Lodge's opinion of the things. He had heard about the photographs before he had ever seen any of them, from the editor of the spiritualist publication *Light*. The photographs had been taken by two Bradford girls, fifteen-year-old Elsie Wright and her cousin, ten-year-old Frances Griffiths, who in 1917 had seen what they described as a goblin and a similar creature. Edward Gardner, a theosophist, had taken the negatives to a specialist photographer who had stated that the pictures had not been touched up or altered in any way and were almost certainly genuine. When Conan Doyle saw the photographs, of dancing goblins and elves in a ring, he suggested that some sort of official inquiry take place. He was told that as the girls had grown up they were reluctant to make too much of what had happened and that their families did not want any publicity at all. Sir Oliver Lodge said that this was all for the best because whatever any photographer might say these photographs were obviously fakes – they looked preposterous. Conan Doyle was shocked. How on earth could two innocent, honest north of England schoolgirls achieve such a thing, and why would they want to in the first place? Too add support to his theory, even Kodak had said that there were no signs of tampering or of superimposition, at least as far as they could tell. Elsie Wright's father also lent credence to the story, explaining that he was sure his camera had not been opened on the day when the photographs were taken and hence nothing underhand could have taken place.

This was where the case had rested until Conan Doyle was handed a letter at the front desk of his Melbourne Hotel; it contained the news that more photographs had now been taken, of flying fairies. Here surely was evidence of the full physical presence of spirits, and why would they not take any form that pleased them, even if it did conform to the popular caricature of what a fairy might look like? Where did this image come from in the first place? Could it not, argued Conan Doyle, be an example of inherited memory or atavistic knowledge? He prepared himself for a fresh spiritualist campaign, on this new subject, when he returned to Britain.

He then moved to New Zealand, where his lectures and meetings in Christchurch were extremely successful. He toured the rest of the South Island and marvelled at its isolation and beauty. From New Zealand the family went to Sri Lanka and then through the Suez Canal and eventually to France. He made the acquaintance of more spiritualists, men and women he had read about but not yet met, and thought that the feeling of fraternity was quite overwhelming. He saw at first hand Eva C., the medium he had heard so much about and defended in his debates and writings in England. He went to one of her seances and was stunned.

'The ectoplasm which I saw upon Eva, the much-abused medium, took the form of a six-inch streak of gelatinous material across the lower portion of the front of the dress. Speaking as a medical man, I should say that it was more like a section of the umbilical chord, but it was wider and softer. I was permitted to touch it, and I felt it thrill and contract between my fingers. It seemed to be breaking through the cloth and to be half embedded in it.' He continued: 'The objection of possible regurgitations of food was made at a very early stage of the investigation,' and concluded: 'it has been met and disproved. So far did Doctor Geley carry his precautions that on one occasion a crimson dye was mixed with Eva's food. In spite of this the ectoplasm was of a luminous white. There is no possible test which has not been applied.'

Back in Britain Conan Doyle spent a further year working for the spiritualist cause and resisted pleas for him to write more fiction and even to provide another collection of Sherlock Holmes stories. His next major work was, not surprisingly, *The Wanderings of a Spiritualist*, published in 1921. At the beginning of the following year the sixty-three-year-old writer clashed with a member of the Society for Psychical Research, Harry Price, and his friends. Price was a sceptic and was especially suspicious and critical of a noted medium in the Midlands, William Hope. He contacted the Imperial Dry Plate Company and bought eight glass plates. Six of them he had treated with X-rays and only he knew of their identity. He then took the marked plates to one of Hope's seances and asked him to take photographs of whatever might occur. As Price had hoped, some of the photographs showed apparently psychic happenings and apparitions, but none of them had been treated with an X-ray. They were different plates and not the product of that evening at all.

Once again Conan Doyle rushed to defend a cause which others thought was hopeless. He argued that X-rays can disappear, particularly if a photographic plate has been overexposed and that, anyway, who was to say that Price and his people had not tampered with the evidence? Was fraud assumed to be practised by only one side in the argument? He suspected plots, libels and conspiracy.

'For twenty-four days after Mr Price takes his packet of marked plates to the headquarters of the SPR it was locked up not in a safe but in an ordinary drawer, which may or may not have been locked, but could presumably. My belief is that during that long period the packet was actually opened and the top plates taken out. Upon one of these top plates of a faked photograph was thrown from one of those small projectors which produced just such an affect as was shown on the returned plate. The ideas may have been that Hope would claim this effect as his own and that he would then be confounded by the announcement that it was there all the time. This was the first stage. The second stage was that either the original conspirator relented or someone else who was in his confidence thought it was too bad, so the packet was again tampered with, the marked and faked plate taken out and a plain one substituted. The packet was then taken to Hope as described. Mr Hope then got a perfectly honest psychic effect upon the unmarked plate. Meanwhile the abstractor, whoever he may have been, had the original faked plate in his possession, and out of pure mischief – for I can imagine no other reason – he wrapped it in a sheet of the College syllabus, which can easily be obtained, and returned it to the SPR, to whom it originally belonged. Wherever it came from it is clear that it did not come from the college, for when a man does a thing secretly and anonymously he does not enclose literature that will lead to his detection.'

It was now time to do more about those fairies he

had thought so much about in Australia. In early 1922 he published an account of the story in *The Coming of the Fairies*. This case had probably done more damage to Conan Doyle's reputation and credibility than any other, perhaps deservedly so. If we look at the photographs today it is difficult to imagine how anybody could have been convinced by them at any time. But convinced they were, and not only Conan Doyle. The case rested on a heavy dose of wishful thinking, spiced with the trusting assumption that the two young girls were above board. In fact it took many years for photographers to develop the equipment and technology to prove that the photographs were fake, and many years for the girls, when grown women, to admit that it was all meant to be a bit of harmless fun.

Around this time Conan Doyle deepened his friendship with another spiritualist. After following her husband into the spiritualist movement Jean told him that she had developed, or perhaps had always had, psychic powers. She managed to make contact with Conan Doyle's son and brother-in-law and with her own brother. One of the first people Conan Doyle rushed to tell was a magician, escapologist and spiritualist dabbler and exposer. Born Erich Weiss in Budapest in 1874, he was now known as Harry Houdini. The two men had first met in 1920 in England and in spite or perhaps because of their very different backgrounds they quickly became close friends. The two of them would wander around London or New York together, arm in arm, this son of Jewish immigrants and the Scottish creator of Sherlock Holmes. Houdini was more interested in the mechanics and the conjuring possibilities of spiritualism than anything else, but he also had a strong sense of religion and a conviction that life did not end with physical death. What did happen when the body gave up he did not know.

Conan Doyle enjoyed his friend's company more than that of most people he knew and he was concerned about his spiritual well-being. He wrote to him: 'I see that you know a great deal about the negative side of spiritualism – I hope more on the positive side will come your way. But it wants to be approached not in the spirit of a detective approaching a suspect, but in that of a humble religious soul yearning for help and comfort.' He continued: 'These clairvoyants, whose names I have given you, are passive agents in themselves and powerless. If left to themselves they guess and muddle – as they sometimes do. When the true connection is formed, all is clear.'

Conan Doyle then invited the naturalized American to stay with his family in England. Jean took to Houdini immediately and later regretted that he had not stayed for longer. Houdini entertained his hosts with tricks and puzzles. Somehow he seemed to be able to pull needles through his cheeks, to produce coins from what seemed to be empty hands. He could escape from locked rooms, per-form acts of hypnosis and accomplish the most astounding of card tricks. He was also witty, able to mimic people and tell wonderful jokes about life in New York. More than all this, he was fascinated by spiritualism. They all discussed the subject long into the night, Conan Doyle and Houdini walking through nearby fields for more than four hours until the sun rose and both men realized that they had missed a night's sleep. Houdini recorded in his diary: 'Visited Sir A. Conan Doyle at Crowborough. Met Lady Doyle and the three children. Had lunch with them. They believe implicitly in spiritualism. Sir Arthur told me he had spoken six times to his son. No possible chance for trickery. Lady Doyle also believed and has tests that are beyond belief. Told them all to me.'

When the Conan Doyles next visited the United States they went to stay with their friend and inevitably the three of them resumed their talks on spiritualism. Conan Doyle was staggered at the size and scope of Houdini's library of the occult and the psychic. There were books that Conan Doyle had never seen, and others he had barely heard of. He became convinced that Houdini had special powers and was almost certainly a medium, maybe a highly important one. At a seance in Atlantic City attended by Houdini and his guests, Jean acted as the medium and almost immediately began to address Houdini with messages from his beloved mother. This was an even more sensitive area for him than one might imagine because he had been trying to make contact with her since her death. Conan Doyle remembered the evening as being tense and dramatic, with his wife writing down pages of notes and handing them to Houdini. After this Houdini himself was given a pencil and paper and spontaneously wrote down the name Dr Ellis Powell, Conan Doyle's old friend and fellow spiritualist campaigner who had recently died in Britain.

Houdini experienced a different evening. He thought that Jean was charming and obliging and certainly wrote down a great deal. The spirit of his mother, however, first signed her letter with a cross and then wrote to her son in English that she had long wanted to talk to him and was overjoyed that she now could. He told everyone present that his mother, a religious Jew, would never have signed anything with the symbol of Christianity and could not write a word of English. At the end of the seance the two men argued and Conan Doyle demanded to know why Houdini would have written the name Powell if the whole evening had been a hoax. Houdini replied that he had simply been thinking of a magician named Powell at the time, that was all.

Houdini went on to write a mocking article about the seance and Conan Doyle was not only hurt by its tone but interpreted it as a personal insult to his wife. He wrote to the man he had trusted and still liked: 'I have no fancy for sparring with a friend in public, so I took no notice. But none the less, I felt rather sore about it. You have all the right in the world to hold your own opinion, but when you say that you have had no evidence of survival, you say what I cannot reconcile with what I saw with my own eyes. I know by many examples the purity of my wife's mediumship, and I saw what you got and what the effect was upon you at the time. You know also that you yourself once wrote down the name of Powell, the one who might be expected to communicate with me. Unless you were joking when you said that you did not know of this Powell's death, then surely that was evidential.'

From this point the relationship between the two men rapidly deteriorated and eventually became hostile and bitter. As for whose fault it was, Houdini was rash and strident when he initially criticized his friend and shouldn't have taken up with Conan Doyle in the first place if he had had in mind to be so destructive of his obviously heartfelt beliefs. Conan Doyle's response was relatively mild and self-controlled. As for why Houdini became so angry over the affair, it was almost certainly because he wanted so very much to believe in what Conan Doyle was saying. Conan Doyle spoke of Houdini shortly before his former friend's death in 1926 and regretted that the two of them had fallen out. It is not known if Houdini felt the same way.

In the United States Conan Doyle's trips and lectures had had a major influence on the formation of spiritualist societies and on provoking discussion in the press of psychic ideas. Because of this excitement *Scientific American* organized a group of experts, including Houdini, to investigate various American mediums, including those whom Conan Doyle had specifically recommended as being bona fide. He did not approve of such a thing, which he described as a witch-hunt disguised an objective analysis.

'The commission is, in my opinion, a farce, and has already killed itself,' he wrote. 'Can people not understand that "psychic" means "of the spirit", and that it concerns not only the invisible spirit of the medium, but equally those of every one of the investigators? A delicate balance and a harmonious atmosphere are needed. I fear some of your recent comments which I have read would not only keep away every decent medium – for they are human beings, not machines, and resent insult – but it would make spirit approach impossible, for they also do not go into an atmosphere which is antagonistic. Thus a certain class of researcher always ruins his result before he begins.'

As he aged Conan Doyle became even more convinced of the truth of his beliefs. He fell out with official spiritualist bodies, argued with individual spiritualists and was openly mocked and parodied but this did not matter to him at all. He built and managed a psychic book shop and museum and acted as a personal information centre for spiritualists the world over. Mediums would stay with him at his home and some of them no doubt exploited his trust and generosity. Yet we cannot dismiss his religious and philosophical ideas as absurd if we wish to retain any intellectual consistency in the study and appreciation of Conan Doyle. A man who was sufficiently gifted and brilliant to invent and develop Sherlock Holmes and Professor Challenger, qualify as a doctor and suggest military reforms far ahead of their time surely did not have one gargantuan weak spot when it came to his personal belief in life after death and the supernatural. We may disagree with him but we would do well also to respect him. He was no extremist and no blind zealot. He understood compromise and moderation.

He wrote, in *In Our African Winter*, shortly before his death: 'I see more clearly that this revelation is the most important that mankind has ever had and that we who are spreading it are doing the most vital work that is done in the world today.' He continued: 'I feel a sympathy with those who desire that the movement should be kept quite unconnected with any creed. It is a broad, noble ideal. But it is not practical and it blocks the way and hinders our advance. If all religions are to be drawn together by this new knowledge there should be two stages, not one, in the process. The first stage should be that each great religion should separately within in its own ranks learn and admit the new revelation. Then the second stage should be that all religions, finding that they have this definite knowledge in common, should draw close to each other. But the first stage is essential, and that is what our leaders have not seen.

NOT FAITH BUT KNOWLEDGE

In a Christian civilisation it is necessary that the personality and ethics of the Christ should be proclaimed in connection with our psychic knowledge, and that the two should be joined together.' He concluded: 'A European spiritualist should in a broad sense be a Christian.' A contemporary student of Arthur Conan Doyle should in a broad sense be a spiritualist.

8

A New Beginning

The years seemed to pass more quickly than they had in the past. Conan Doyle told Jean that his body simply would not do what it was told any more. She smiled and then so did he. He wasn't at all afraid of death and in many ways looked forward to it as the next great step in life. Not that he was passively waiting for it. He travelled as much as ever but wrote less. His energy was still remarkable and his working hours were as long as ever. There was one more trip to Canada, that country he so liked, in 1923, and once again he took advantage of his time in a different country to meet with local spiritualists. In a deliciously representative, typical and touchingly naive piece, he wrote about an encounter he had in Winnipeg. It is worth quoting at length.

'The man who goes upon occult paths does certainly have an extraordinary variety of experience. Let me briefly narrate that which happened on the morning of July 4th. The day after my lecture at Winnipeg, which had been a remarkably successful one to a very crowded house, I had heard of a strange circle and of a very remarkable medium whom I will call Mrs Bolton. At 9am one of her devotees, who are absolutely wholehearted in their belief and devotion, was at the hotel door with a car. After a four mile drive we alighted at a lonely villa on the extreme outskirts of the town, where there were six other men and three women to meet us.

The men were all alert, middle-aged or young, evidently keen men of business who might have been accountants or merchants. Yet here they were from 10.00 onwards on a working day giving themselves up to what was in their eyes infinitely more important than business.

'We sat around the room, and presently Mrs Bolton entered, a woman of the Blavatsky type of rounded face, but less heavy. She seemed gentle and amiable. She sat down while "Lead Kindly Light" was sung. Then she sank into a trance, from which she quietly emerged with an aspect of very great dignity and benevolence. I have never seen more commanding eyes than those which fixed us in turn. "It is the Master. It is the High Spirit," whispered my neighbours. Standing up and greeting each of us in turn, the medium, or the entity controlling her, proceeded to baptise a child nine weeks old belonging to one of the circle. The mother might have stood for a model of reverence and awe. She then handed round bread and wine as in the Sacrament. The wine, I was assured by all, was simply water drawn from the domestic supply. It had now become faintly red with an aromatic odour and taste. At every meeting this miracle of changing the water into wine was performed, according to the unanimous testimony of these very same workaday men of the world, who declared that they themselves had drawn the water. I could not give a name to the taste and smell, which were very pleasant. It was certainly non-alcoholic.

'We then had a long address, which was in the medium's own voice and dialect, but purported to come from the high control. My growing deafness made me miss some of it, but what I heard was dignified and impressive. After speaking for nearly an hour, a second control took possession. He was more smiling and homely but less majestic and dignified than the higher one. The latter, by the way, unbent in a very charming way when he blessed the little boy who was present, saying "I remember when I was a little boy myself once." The second control gave messages relating to worldly things relating to several of the circle, who received them with deep reverence. They assured me that they never failed to be true. He spoke of conditions at death. "The dark valley on the other side waits for all. I am in the glorious city at the end. Those who are prepared by knowledge, as you are, soon pass the Valley. But some linger very long."

'Then after some ceremonies which I may not describe the seance ended and Mrs Bolton, the plain, homely, uneducated Lancashire woman, came back into her own body. What is one to say about such a performance? It was against all my prepossessions, for I have a deep distrust of ritual and form and sacraments, and here were all these things; yet they were solemn and moving, and nothing can exceed the absolute faith of these men and women. Their faith is founded, as they assured me, upon long experience in which they have seen miracle after miracle including materialisation of these high personages. I cannot claim that I saw anything evidential with my own eyes, and yet I am convinced that my informant was speaking truth as far as he saw it, when he claimed that he poured water into the chalice and that it had been transformed. It all left me with mixed feelings, but the conviction that I had been on the fringe of something very sacred and solemn was predominant. It is true that these high Spirits occasionally use Lancashire speech, but as one of them said, "We cannot open brain cells which have never been opened. We have to use what is there."

'When I consider the wonderful psychical phenomena of the one circle seen with my own eyes and the religious atmosphere of the other, I came away with the conclusion that Winnipeg stands very high among the places we have visited for its psychic possibilities.'

But there was more to do than attend seances. Sport had always been an obsession of Conan Doyle's and he had a soft spot for that least English of games, baseball. 'We came upon it on Dominion Day, when all business was suspended and everyone was in festivity, so we fitted ourselves into the picture and attended an international baseball match between Winnipeg and Indianapolis in the morning. Both sides seemed to me to be surprisingly good and the fielding, catching and throwing-in were far superior to that of good English cricket teams. Of course in catching they are aided by the great glove on the left hand, but every cricketer knows the difficulty of judging a long catch, and when I say that not one was misjudged or dropped by either side out of at least fifty, it will show how high was the standard. I wish more and more that this game could acclimatise in Britain, for it has many points which make it the ideal game both for players and spectators. I have all the prejudices of an old cricketer, and yet I cannot get away from the fact that baseball is the better game.'

Such was his character that when he returned home to Britain he wrote to various newspapers spreading the good news of baseball and explaining how it was the game of the future. His letter-writing was ceaseless. Any subject of interest seemed to merit a letter to a newspaper, from local and religious publications to the great nationals. He would usually begin his letter-writing in the early morning after he had read the newspapers. It was cathartic and enjoyable for him to let off steam and pronounce on any subject he thought fit, from horse-racing to photography, Scottish nationalism to country dancing. He would often write out his letters a second time so as to keep a personal record that was in perfect condition. He also replied to as much mail as he could and took trouble over small requests and questions. Some of his letters were trivial, others more significant. In late November 1927, for example, he wrote to the *Morning Post* on the subject of habitual criminals. 'I think that our admirable Home Secretary opened up a most important line of thought when he suggested that the habitual criminal should be treated as the abnormal man that he is, and *never* let loose upon the community.

'If a man has been in prison, let us say, six times for violent assault, and then commits yet another one, on whom does the guilt lie, on the man or on the authority who set him free? I should say the latter, since the man may not be master

187

of his own actions, but the release of so dangerous a person is deliberate.

'Let us suppose that an annexe was built to the Dartmoor Prison, and that the really hopeless criminals were gradually segregated there after they had served their ordinary term. Their conditions might be those of comparative comfort, but there should be no question of release. By the time you had 1000 in this cage imagine the relief it would be to the police force and the courts. There is also the question of eugenics, and that of the contamination of the young by the example of the hardened crook.' And then in a final, telling and ominous sentence: 'It would take a rather ruthless man to carry the matter through, but there are times when ruthlessness to some means kindness to others.'

There were more booklets and pamphlets but none was more eagerly awaited than *The Case-Book of Sherlock Holmes*. This is arguably the weakest of the Holmes collections and was written in something of a hurry, with less enthusiasm than had been injected into the writing of the earlier stories. The last set of Holmes tales appeared in 1927, published by John Murray in Britain and by George H. Doran in the United States. The collection consisted of 'The Adventure of the Illustrious Client', 'The Adventure of the Blanched Soldier', 'The Adventure of the Mazarin Stone', 'The Adventure of the Three Gables', 'The Adventure of the Sussex Vampire', 'The Adventure of the Three Garridebs', 'The Problem of Thor Bridge', 'The Adventure of the Creeping Man', 'The Adventure of the Lion's Mane', 'The Adventure of the Veiled Lodger', 'The Adventure of Shoscombe Old Place' and 'The Adventure of the Retired Colourman'. A great many adventures and only one problem. More than one problem actually, because several of the stories do not do Conan Doyle or Sherlock Holmes justice.

'The Adventure of the Illustrious Client' is one of the better stories, darker and crueller than most. The eponymous client is never identified but convinces Holmes to take the case, to dissuade a wealthy and attractive young woman from marrying or even continuing her relationship with a Baron Gruner. Holmes is told by his employer that Gruner is a disreputable and exploitative man, capable of almost any crime. Holmes attempts to persuade the young woman but she is devoted to Gruner and dismisses the detective's story with contempt and anger. The case is concluded by the intervention of one Kitty Winter, herself wronged in the past by Bruner. She throws vitriol in Gruner's face, providing one of the more violent examples of Conan Doyle's divine and natural justice episodes. During the attempt to save the woman from the evil baron, however, Holmes receives a rare and bloody beating at the hands of his enemies. Watson learns of the attack in a newspaper article headed 'Murderous Attack Upon Sherlock Holmes'. The faithful friend writes: 'I think I stood stunned for moments. Then I have a confused recollection of snatching at a paper, of the remonstrance of the man, whom I had not paid, and, finally, of standing in the doorway of a chemist's shop while I turned up the fateful paragraph. This was how it ran: We learn with regret that Mr Sherlock Holmes, the well-known private detective, was the victim this morning of a murderous assault which has left him in a precarious position. There are no exact details to hand, but the event seems to have occurred about twelve o'clock in Regent Street, outside the Cafe Royal. The attack was made by three armed men with sticks, and Mr Holmes was beaten about the head and body, receiving injuries which the doctors describe as most serious. He was carried to Charing Cross Hospital, and afterwards insisted upon being taken to his rooms in Baker Street. The miscreants who attacked him appear to have been respectably dressed men, who escaped from the bystanders by passing through the Cafe Royal and out into Glasshouse Street behind it. No doubt they belonged to that criminal fraternity which had so often had occasion to bewail the activity and ingenuity of the injured man.'

'The Problem of Thor Bridge' is a pure detection story. Holmes manages to explain the perplexing death of one

Maria Gibson by discovering a dent in a stone bridge. The plot involves lost love and the falsely accused. The solution to the story's problem is among the best and crispiest in the canon. 'Then she took one of her husband's revolvers – there was, as you saw, an arsenal in the house – and kept it for her own use. A similar one she concealed that morning in Miss Dunbar's wardrobe after discharging one barrel, which she could easily do in the woods without attracting attention. She then went down to the bridge where she had contrived this exceedingly ingenious method of getting rid of her weapon. When Miss Dunbar appeared she used her last breath in pouring out her hatred, and then, when she was out of hearing, carried out her terrible purpose. Every link is now in its place and the chain is complete. The papers may ask why the mere was not dragged in the first instance, but it is easy to be wise after the event, and in any case the expanse of a reed-filled lake is no easy matter to drag unless you have a clear perception of what you are looking for an where. Well, Watson, we have helped a remarkable woman and also a formidable man . . .'

To be wise after the event. Holmes would not have been so forgiving and understanding in the past. There are other attitudes in this last collection that are not to be found in the earlier stories. There is a flavour of decline in the collection, hints of pain and suffering, well demonstrated in 'The Adventures of the Lion's Mane', where Conan Doyle writes in one memorable passage: 'His back was covered with dark red lines as though he had been terribly flogged by a thin wine scourge. The instrument with which this punishment had been inflicted was clearly flexible, for the long, angry weals curved round his shoulders and ribs. There was blood dripping down his chin, for he had bitten through his lower lip in the paroxysm of his agony. His drawn and distorted face told how terrible that agony had been.' This is, in fact, one of the few stories where Holmes rather than Watson is the narrator of the tale, although the style, approach and pacing is almost identical to that of

Conan Doyle as Watson. Here Holmes has retired to the Sussex coast but is obliged to investigate the death of Fitzroy McPherson. The death is solved as being due not to crime but to a natural occurrence, but the story does bring us the 'most complete and remarkable woman', Maud Bellamy.

'The Adventure of the Blanched Soldier' takes as its theme the consequences of the Boer War, that conflict so close to Conan Doyle's heart. The author also relied on his medical training as well as war experiences in a South African military hospital for the story, which concerns an ex-soldier whose family assume him to have a fatal disease. There is too little detection and too little characterization for this story to succeed.

'The Adventure of the Mazarin Stone' is an even less impressive piece of work, regarded by many as the most disappointing story in the entire Holmes collection. It is also exceptional because it is written in the third person, without Watson as the narrator of the story, largely because it is an adaptation of a play about Sherlock Holmes called *The Crown Diamond*, written by Conan Doyle some years earlier and produced for the stage in 1921.

'The Adventure of the Three Gables' is a superior piece, another story where Holmes enters the world of sex, black-mail and intrigue. Here a young man becomes infatuated with an elder woman and a strong female character, Isadora Klein, is a central part of the tale. One passage early in the story involves the appearance of a black man, a rare occurrence in a Conan Doyle book. The description is crass but not untypical of the era. 'The door had flown open and a huge negro had burst into the room. He would have been a comic figure if he had not been terrific, for he was dressed in a very loud grey check suit with a flowing salmon-coloured tie. His broad face and flattened nose were thrust forward, as his sullen dark eyes, with a smouldering gleam of malice in them, turned from one of us to the other.

'"Which of you gentleman is Masser Holmes?" he asked.

'Holmes raised his pipe with a languid smile.

"'Oh! it's you, is it?" said our visitor, coming with an unpleasant, stealthy step round the angle of the table. "See here, Masser Holmes, you keep your hands out of other folks' business. Leave folks to manage their own affairs. Got that, Masser Holmes?"'

Conan Doyle also refers to the character as a 'savage' in the piece. When the story was published its author received a letter from a black reader in the United States explaining that he was disappointed in Conan Doyle, a man of such forward thinking and progressive thoughts. Could not, he asked, the creator of Sherlock Holmes have written a more sensitive portrayal of a black man, particularly as he had already shown his racial understanding and tolerance in the Congo case and elsewhere. It is to Conan Doyle's credit that he replied in contrite tones, explaining that if he ever wrote again of a man of 'this race and colour' he would try to be far more empathetic.

'The Adventure of the Sussex Vampire' contains the curious incident of the bloodsucker on England's south coast. But, one replies, there was no bloodsucker on the south coast. That was the curious incident. There is no monster here at all but a firmly and entertainingly explained account of a South American woman in a small village and local superstition.

'The Adventure of the Three Garridebs' is ostensibly not about the solution of a crime but the search for men who share the strange surname of the title. When the three are found they are to share a fortune. As is obvious from the outset, the entire Garrideb escape is contrived and merely a plot, much as was the Red-Headed League in that earlier magnificent story. In fact the tale owes just a little too much to that gem in *The Adventures of Sherlock Holmes*. Yet it still contains the occasional moment of sheer Sherlockian magic, mingling anticipation of the chase with eccentricity and depth of character.

'I remember the date very well, for it was in the same month that Holmes refused a knighthood for services which may perhaps some day be described. I only refer to the matter in passing, for in my position of partner and confidant I am obliged to be particularly careful to avoid any indiscretion. I repeat, however, that this enables me to fix the date, which was the latter end of June, 1902, shortly after the conclusion of the South African war. Holmes had spent several days in bed, as was his habit from time to time, but he emerged that morning with a long foolscap document in his hand and a twinkle of amusement in his austere grey eyes.'

'The Adventure of the Creeping Man' borders on science fiction. The strange behaviour of a professor is eventually explained by Holmes, who discovers that the man is injecting into himself serum from monkeys. Daring for its time, the story now reads far too anachronistically and is comical rather than terrifying or mysterious. But it is strong on Sherlockian atmosphere and is particularly helpful in enlightening the relationship between Holmes and Watson. 'It was one Sunday evening early in September of the year 1903 that I received one of Holmes's laconic messages; "Come at once if convenient – if inconvenient come all the same – SH." The relations between us in those latter days were peculiar. He was a man of habits, narrow and concentrated habits, and I had become one of them. As an institution I was like the violin, the shag tobacco, the old black pipe, the index books, and others perhaps less excusable. When it was a case of active work and a comrade was needed upon whose nerve he could place some reliance, my role was obvious. But apart from this I had uses. I was a whetstone for his mind. I stimulated him. He liked to think aloud in my presence. His remarks could hardly be said to be made to me – many of them would have been as appropriately addressed to his bedstead – but none the less, having formed the habit, it had become in some way helpful that I should register and interject. If I irritated him by a certain methodical slowness in my mentality, that irritation served only to make his own flame-like intuitions and impressions flash up the more vividly and swiftly. Such was my humble role in our alliance.

'When I arrived at Baker Street I found him huddled up in his arm-chair with updrawn knees, his pipe in his mouth and his brow furrowed with thought. It was clear that he was in the throes of some vexatious problem. With a wave of his hand he indicated my old arm-chair, but otherwise for half an hour he gave no sign that he was aware of my presence. Then with a start he seemed to come from his reverie, and, with his usual whimsical smile, he greeted me back to what had once been my home.'

In 'The Adventure of the Veiled Lodger' Conan Doyle simply poured out his thoughts on a set of subjects close to his heart and has his detective proclaim rather than detect. His editors asked that he replace the story with another but the request was declined. Yet there are still some occasional insights into Holmes. 'When one considers that Mr Sherlock Holmes was in active practice for twenty-three years, and that during seventeen of these I was allowed to co-operate with him and to keep notes of his doings, it would be clear that I have a mass of material at my command. The problem has always been, not to find, but to choose. There is the long row of year-books which fill a shelf, and there are the dispatch-cases filled with documents, a perfect quarry for the student not only of crime, but of the social and official scandals of the late Victorian era. Concerning these latter, I may say that the writers of agonized letters, who begged that the honour of their families or the reputation of famous forebears may not be touched, have nothing to fear. The discretion and high sense of professional honour which have always distinguished my friend are still at work in the choice of these memoirs, and no confidant will be abused. I deprecate, however, in the strongest way the attempts which have been made lately to get at and destroy these papers.' 'The source of these outrages is known, and if they are repeated I have Mr Holmes's authority for saying that the whole story concerning the politician, the lighthouse, and the chained cormorant will be given to the public. There is at least one reader who will understand.'

Originally the entire canon of Sherlock Holmes stories concluded with 'The Adventure of Shoscombe Old Place', but later editions made it the penultimate tale. It is fitting that this Holmes story should have been written so late – it originally appeared in the *Strand Magazine* in April 1927 – and that it concerns death and graveyards. There is no real crime in the story – only a fraud and a clever piece of detection involving a dog being able to identify a person when a human being cannot.

'The Adventure of the Retired Colourman' appeared in the *Strand* in January 1927 and is remembered in part as the only story in the whole series containing a reference to chess – surprising given Holmes's frame of mind and line of reasoning. Conan Doyle had learnt the game when he was a boy and went through periods of either revelling in it – on board ship when he was a young man and later, during the Boer War – or despising it as a confused, confusing waste of time. Friends thought that his attitude depended on how well he had performed in the previous half dozen games.

The tale, and the stories of Sherlock Holmes, end with the following: 'It is generally known now that this singular episode ended upon a happier note than Sir Robert's actions deserved. Shoscombe Prince did win the Derby, the sporting owner did net £80,000 in bets, and the creditors did hold their hand until the race was over, when they were paid in full, and enough was left to reestablish Sir Robert in a fair position in life. Both police and coroner took a lenient view of the transaction, and beyond a mild censure for the delay in registering the lady's decease, the lucky owner got away scatheless from the strange incident in a career which has now outlived its shadows and promises to end in an honoured old age.' Conan Doyle knew that there would be no more of Sherlock Holmes from his pen.

There were more trips now, even though Conan Doyle's

friends and doctors advised against it. He was known to have dizzy spells, to lose some of the feeling in his right leg and to sleep badly. To travel abroad would be foolish and dangerous, he was advised. Nonsense, replied Conan Doyle, the new air would do him good and the excitement and adventure of travel would be rejuvenating. In the autumn of 1928 he set sail for South Africa, Kenya and Rhodesia, accompanied by Jean and the three children. Denis and Adrian were grown now but they still showed a respect for, even an awe of their father. He still told them how to behave and was prepared to chastise them, physically if necessary, if they broke what was to him a sacred if unwritten law of good manners, social order, masculine virtue and integrity. They were never frightened of their father but they always knew when it was best not to argue with him. This could be difficult in Conan Doyle's latter years because with his growing deafness he would sometimes be convinced that he had heard his children make remarks that they certainly had not made. It was just father, they said. They knew him. More to the point, they loved him.

The South Africa which greeted Conan Doyle was a very different country from the one he had left all those years ago during the Boer War. He still harboured a certain resentment of the way the South Africans had tried to paint British soldiers as murderers and butchers but he was unaware that many South Africans still saw him as a propagandist for British imperialism and a defender of concentration camps and the killing of women and children. Although most of the people Conan Doyle met on the trip were friendly and enthusiastic he also encountered coldness, dislike and even, in Cape Town, a small demonstration against his visit. But the trip was not meant to be political, even though he could not restrain himself when a remotely political question was asked at a press conference. For the most part he spoke to small and medium-sized groups about spiritualism, was interviewed by the press about Sherlock

Holmes and chatted to old friends about the second coming of the German menace.

The latter was increasingly on Conan Doyle's mind in 1928 and 1929. He was sure that after the Armistice the German nation could never rise up to challenge Britain or its allies again. But he now thought differently. His regular correspondence with spiritualist friends in Berlin and Munich was now filled less with matters psychic than with matters political. They told him that the country was polarized as never before and that there seemed to be no longer any alternative but some form of extremism. A good number of Conan Doyle's German friends were Jewish and one, as early as 1929, asked if he could send his family to stay with Conan Doyle before applying to live permanently in Britain. It is fascinating to speculate as to what Conan Doyle, the ever-vigilant champion of justice, would have done if he had been a younger man. As it was, he wrote to friends who were in Parliament, arranged for his refugee friend to find a home in London and delivered a small series of public lectures, 'The Future of Europe', stressing the tenuous position of the Jews. If Britain was to be in any sort of position to do anything at all for anybody, he said, she must concentrate on building her armed forces and must look to mechanized warfare as the style of the future.

In 1929 he decided to visit Scandinavia and Holland, travelling to The Hague, Copenhagen and Stockholm. He spoke on the radio, visited the monuments of former glories and past wars and was greeted by large and adoring crowds. In those countries they read Sherlock Holmes in English but, to Conan Doyle's surprise and delight, they enjoyed local translations of his spiritualist writings. He liked Scandinavia, felt comfortable in its clean, almost pristine forests and its organized cities. In Norway he was asked about *Pheneas Speaks*, which had appeared in 1927. This book has deceased friends of Conan Doyle returning to life and confirming that everything he had thought and written about spiritualism was accurate and authentic. 'England is to be the centre to which all humanity will turn,' he wrote in the scathingly reviewed volume. 'She is to be the beacon of light in this dark, dark world' and 'Things are already working, but the human eye cannot see it. In a storm you only hear a far-off rumble at first, and then it comes on and on till it is roaring overhead.' Conan Doyle's mother spoke in the book, assuring her son that all would be well and that God would make sure that the newspapers were not so cynical and rude to her son and his spiritualist religion. For some reason the Norwegians were rather taken by all this.

Another book, *The Maracot Deep and Other Stories*, had appeared in 1929, and it would have been better for all concerned had the wretched work never appeared. This was supposed to be another book in the genre of *The Lost World* but it had none of that work's charm or style. One character in it, Scanlan, speaks in a manner that may have been based on Conan Doyle's former friend Houdini but the author has no ear for the nuances of working-class New York and the dialogue from this unfortunate man is a bad hybrid of Runyon and Bunyan. The intrepid explorers travel to the bottom of the Atlantic in a diving-bell but the device snaps from its cable and falls beneath the seabed. Just as the occupants prepare for their death they are rescued and taken to an underground city. The rescuers are descendants of the men and women of Atlantis and are now divided into two distinct races, one composed of large Caucasians, the other diminutive Negroes. In true Wellsian style the city is in some ways more advanced than that from which the rescued party originated, with synthetic and healthy food, telepathic communication and many of the more trite creations projected by science-fiction writers in the 1920s as being the stuff of the future. An important aspect of the book is the description of its central character, Maracot. 'The long, thin, aggressive nose, the two small gleaming grey eyes set closely together under a thatch of eyebrows, the thin-lipped, compressed mouth, the cheeks worn into hollows by constant thought and ascetic life, are all uncompanionable. He lives on some mental mountain-top, out of reach of ordinary mortals.' There is little doubt that this was the last appearance of Sherlock Holmes and it is possible that Maracot's foe, the Lord of the Dark Face, was Professor Moriarty. The two men meet and the successor to Moriarty boasts that he will destroy the world. Instead Maracot destroys him. Within this post-Sherlockian story are moral warnings about the banality of any future age that might numb its inhabitants into a safe but ultimately pointless existence, and depictions of wild and wonderful creatures from Conan Doyle's imagination.

Of the other stories in the book the best is 'When the World Screamed', not least for its title. Conan Doyle was particularly proud of this one, featuring as it does his beloved Professor Challenger being convinced that the world is a living organism, drilling an enormous hole and finding a breathing, shining mass of substance at the heart of the planet. One of his companions thrusts a harpoon into what is found and the planet lets out a gigantic, shattering shout. 'She voiced her indignation,' wrote Conan Doyle.

He was still writing letters, even though he sometimes needed the help of a secretary and a special desk that had been designed by a carpenter friend and was at just the correct height and shape to ease his worsening back and neck pain. He once said that the art of letter-writing was perhaps the most noble and least polished in all of the literary genre. He enjoyed the direct contact it gave him with the public, and relished the broad scope his fame now allowed him in writing about anything he wanted to any of the major newspapers of the day. How spoilt I am, he said, and how much the letters pages will miss my obsessions and eccentricities when I am gone. On 6 March 1930 he wrote to the *Morning Post* of a 'Strange Experience'.

'In the early morning of February 3 I was lying awake when I became aware of heavy steps approaching along the passage which leads to my room. They were quite as well marked as those of the butler when he brings me my early morning cup of tea. They paused outside my door, and I then heard clearly a short cough as of someone clearing their throat.

'I turned up the light and noticed that it was 3.30 a.m. I then rose and went to the door. I flung it open fully expecting to find some person on the other side. The light from my lamp shone down the passage and there was no one there. Having made sure that this was the case, I returned to bed in a somewhat shaken state, as I was a sick man and in no condition for such nocturnal adventures.

'In a quarter of an hour or so my heart palpitation passed away and I fell into a deep sleep.

'Two days later my wife received a letter from Mrs Osborne Leonard, the well-known medium, saying that she had never dreamt of me before in her life, but that between 3.30 and four o'clock on Monday morning she had had an extraordinarily vivid impression of having visited me and actually seeing me and administering some healing treatment to me. "It was all so real," she said, "that it cannot be classed as a dream." In this letter Mrs Leonard offered to come to Crowborough and to give me a special seance, which she did three days later nobly fulfilling her promise, which involved a drive of thirty miles partly through deep snow.

'The seance was a very wonderful experience, but it makes a story by itself. When it was over I discussed with Mrs Leonard the happenings of Monday morning, and I mentioned to her the short cough which I had heard outside my door. She said: "That is really final. I seldom have anything the matter with my throat, but that night every time I woke I found myself coughing in the very way you describe. It was so unusual that it impressed itself upon my memory."

'These are the facts, and they seem to me beyond all range of coincidence, and to present a very clear case of bi-location. Mrs Leonard was sleeping at Kenley but undoubtedly her double or etheric body had visited me at Crowborough.'

The wishful thinking of a man who knew that death could

not be very far away or another vision by Conan Doyle of the supernatural? The letter provoked a passionate response, both from supporters and opponents. A drunken butler or a broken clock, said some; definitely a visit from beyond, said others, and one letter to Conan Doyle went so far as to explain that he had without doubt been visited by an angel or suchlike and had received an advanced notice of his death. Conan Doyle was not particularly comforted.

Indeed comfort was in short supply now. By the time he had returned from Europe his health was obviously not good and, unlike previous problems, there seemed to be no major recovery now. He was coughing a great deal and found it difficult to sleep. He was also restless and, unusual for him, irritable. He would come through one small problem and another would develop. It all seemed surmountable. I seem, he said, to be winding down like some old clock that has done its bit. Immediately he had come back to Britain he had complained of cramp in his arm and had walked around the room thrusting his shoulder up and down to relieve the pain. He must have been in something approaching agony, because Conan Doyle did not complain about pain very often. The next day he had a heart attack. Doctors, family and friends rushed to his side but after a brief stay in hospital he was allowed home. He had been lucky, he was told, and should take this attack as a warning. Slow down, take things easy, because there would be no more such warnings. Nonsense, he replied, I am a doctor and I learnt the speech about the heart attack warning along with every other medical student. He was out of bed, walking in the garden and writing notes and letters far too quickly. I feel better every day, he said.

By November even the doctors agreed with him, so he was given permission – he would not have cared even had he not been given it – to attend the Armistice Day Memorial Service, speak at the Royal Albert Hall in the afternoon and at the Queen's Hall in the evening. As he prepared his speeches for the event the emotion of it all, and the memories of his son and brother, seemed to pierce at his very soul. He shook as he wrote and then rehearsed his speech. Cancel now, he was advised. No, never. He spoke at all his engagements, even though it was snowing and a strong, cold wind chilled even healthy young people to the bone. He stood on a balcony wearing only a suit and a thin coat and addressed an approving crowd. As he did so the snow fell upon his shoulders and melted down his face from his hair. He went home and, for the first time, told Jean that perhaps it would be best if he did not attend the following year's service.

The next day he could not get out of bed by himself. Once out he was reluctant to get back in. My recovery is being hindered and not improved by all this fuss, he said. I will sleep and rest when I want to sleep and rest. He ventured one last time out into the changing world, to meet and discuss, of course, spiritualism. He talked about his last book, *The Edge of the Unknown*, a collection of fifteen spiritualist essays, ranging from 'The Riddle of Houdini' to 'A New Light on Old Crimes'. The preface, written from his bed in Crowborough, is especially poignant. 'There is a passage in that charming book *The Bridge of San Luis Rey* which runs as follows: "She was one of these persons who have allowed their lives to be gnawed away because they have fallen in love with an idea several centuries before its appointed appearance in the history of Civilization. She hurled herself against the obstinacy of her time." We who believe in the psychic revelation, and who appreciate that a perception of these things is of the utmost importance, certainly have hurled ourselves against the obstinacy of our time. Possibly we have allowed some of our lives to be gnawed away in what, for the moment, seemed a vain and thankless quest. Only the future can show whether the sacrifice was worth it. Personally I think that it was. Among the various chords which are struck in this little book there may be some to which the mind will respond, and which may entice him also in the search for the Holy Grail.'

It was the Holy Grail that was now in sight. That last

outing should never have happened and Conan Doyle had to be taken home again, unable to move and barely able to speak. He was being given oxygen now and Jean was weeping by his bed. The morning of 7 July 1930 came with sun and warmth. Conan Doyle asked for his bedroom window to be opened so that he could hear the birds sing. His room was him: boxing gloves, pictures of Regency boxers, a portrait of Sherlock Holmes. He was ready. He knew it. So did Jean. He comforted his family, told them that it was more difficult for them than it was for him and that he knew they would all meet again. Death did not frighten him because it was not really death at all. He could hardly be understood now but Jean realized from signals and gestures that her husband wanted to sit in his armchair. She got him there, sat him down and held his hand. At 8.30 that morning the seventy-one-year-old Arthur Conan Doyle, knight of the realm, laid his head back on his pillow and squeezed his beloved wife's hand. She knew that he had just entered through a very large door into a world that we can only imagine.

The funeral was held four days later and the attending crowd did the man justice. Conan Doyle had asked that there be no mourning and for the most part his wishes were obeyed. There were, of course, letters of condolence from all over the world and Jean and the children felt proud as they read them. It was a warm, fine day and the flowers were in bloom. He would have liked that. He would also have liked the headstone, made from British oak and as simple and gracious as Conan Doyle. 'Steel true, blade straight,' said the inscription. Perhaps others might have remembered him from an earlier death that did not turn out to be quite that. They would have recalled Dr Watson's words written all those years ago about Sherlock Holmes. He was, said the faithful friend, 'the best and the wisest man whom I have ever known'. Perhaps he was.

Sources

1: A Scottish Childhood

1 *Memories and Adventures*, Conan Doyle
2 Ibid.
3 Ibid.
4 Ibid.
5 Ibid.
6 G.K. Chesterton papers, British Library
7 *Memories and Adventures*
8 G.K. Chesterton papers
9 *Memories and Adventures*

2: Doctoring and Deception

1 Portsmouth Libraries
2 *Memories and Adventures*, Conan Doyle
3 Ibid.
4 Ibid.
5 Portsmouth Libraries
6 G.K. Chesterton papers, British Library
7 Ibid.
8 *Memories and Adventures*

3: Bohemia and Beyond

1 *Memories and Adventures*, Conan Doyle
2 Ibid.
3 *John O'London's Weekly*, 19 April 1919
4 G.K. Chesterton papers, British Library
5 Central Zionist Archives, Jerusalem, File A120/331
6 G.K. Chesterton papers

4: To Defend What is Right

1 G.K. Chesterton papers, British Library
2 *Memories and Adventures*, Conan Doyle

SOURCES

3 Ibid.
4 Author

5: The Real-Life Detective

1 *Omnibus Edition* of long Sherlock Holmes stories, 1929
2 *Memories and Adventures*, Conan Doyle
3 Ibid.
4 Conan Doyle to G.K. Chesterton, G.K. Chesterton papers, British Library

6: A Crime Exposed

1 G.K. Chesterton papers, British Library

7: Not Faith But Knowledge

1 Author's interview with Julian Symons
2 *Two Worlds Christmas Supplement*, 19 December 1919
3 Ibid.
4 *History of Spiritualism*, 1926

Bibliography

Many of the papers and letters of Arthur Conan Doyle are, unfortunately, not yet available to the public or open to any researchers or biographers. There are documents in the British Library in London, and in Edinburgh, Texas, Toronto and Portsmouth. It may be that within a generation all of the papers will be available and most of them collected in one location.

By far the best edition of the Sherlock Holmes stories is *The Oxford Sherlock Holmes*, the general editor being Owen Dudley Edwards. One of the individual editors is Christopher Roden, who is also the founder of the Arthur Conan Doyle Society, the first group to take a serious interest in Conan Doyle rather than one of his fictional creations.

Of the numerous books published about Conan Doyle and Sherlock Holmes many are best left alone. Some of the best include the following:

Baring-Gould, W.S., *Sherlock Holmes, a Biography*, 1962
Bell, Joseph, *Mr Sherlock Holmes*, 1893
Brend, G. *My Dear Holmes*, 1951
Broad, C.D., *Religion, Philosophy, and Psychic Research*, 1953
Carr, John Dickson, *The Life of Sir Arthur Conan Doyle*, 1949
Dilnot, G., *Scotland Yard*, 1926
Edwards, Owen Dudley, *The Quest for Sherlock Holmes*, 1983
Gatenby, Greg, *The Wild is Always There*, 1993

BIBLIOGRAPHY

Gibson, John Michael & Lancelyn Green, Richard, *Letters to the Press*, 1986

Gordon, H., *The War Office*, 1935

Gruggen, Rev. G. and Keating, J., *Stonyhurst*, 1901

Hardwick, M. and M., *The Man Who Was Sherlock Holmes*, 1964

Henslow, G., *Truths of Spiritualism*, 1919

Higham, Charles, *The Adventures of Conan Doyle*, 1976

Hill, J. Arthur, *Letters from Sir Oliver Lodge*, 1932

Holroyd, J.E., *Baker Street Byways*, 1959

Horn, D.B., *Short History of the University of Edinburgh*, 1967

Inglis, Brian, *Roger Casement*, 1973

Jerome, Jerome K., *My Life and Times*, 1926

Jones, Kelvin I., *Conan Doyle and the Spirits*, 1989

Lamond, John, *Arthur Conan Doyle*, 1931

Lellenberg, Jon L., *The Quest for Sir Arthur Conan Doyle*, 1987

Lodge, Oliver, *Survival of Man*, 1920

Lodge, Oliver, *Past Years*, 1931

MacCabe, Joseph, *Is Spiritualism Based on Fraud?*, 1920

Nordon, Pierre, *Sir Arthur Conan Doyle*, 1964

Pearsall, Ronald, *Conan Doyle: A Biographical Solution*, 1977

Pearson, Hesketh, *Conan Doyle*, 1943

Pointer, Michael, *The Public Life of Sherlock Holmes*, 1975

Redmond, Christopher, *A Sherlock Holmes Handbook*, 1993

Redmond, Donald A., *Sherlock Holmes: A Study in Sources*, 1982

Roughhead, W., *The Trial of Oscar Slater*, 1929

Starrett, V., *The Private Life of Sherlock Holmes*, 1934

Symons, Julian, *Conan Doyle: Portrait of an Artist*, 1979

Tracey, Jack, *The Encyclopaedia Sherlockiana*, 1977

Warrack, Guy, *Sherlock Holmes and Music*, 1947

Index

INDEX

INDEX